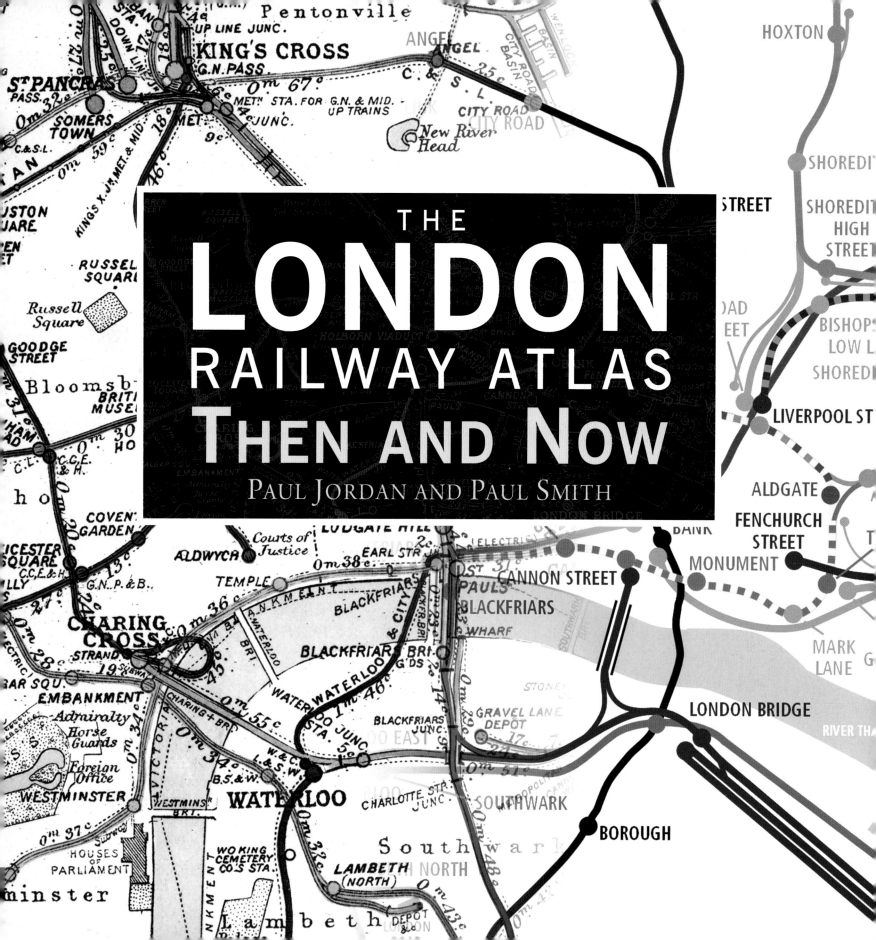

THE
LONDON
RAILWAY ATLAS
THEN AND NOW

Paul Jordan and Paul Smith

Ex-GWR 1400 Class 0-4-2T No.1436 at **Drayton Green Halt** *(See Map 21)* on June 3rd, 1956. The station was opened by the GWR in 1905 and renamed as *Drayton Green* by BR on May 5th, 1969.   *Marcus Eavis/Online Transport Archive*

First published by Crécy Publishing Ltd 2016

© Paul Jordan & Paul Smith 2016

A CIP record for this book is available from the British Library

ISBN 9781908 347435

Legends for photographs on the back of the jacket cover, clockwise from top left;

Class 395 "Javelin" EMU No.395006 awaiting departure from **St Pancras International station** on August 30th, 2011.

Looking north at **Carpenders Park station** on March 30th, 1974.   *Alan Young*

Class 466 EMU No.466012 on Platform 6 at **London Bridge station** on April 20th, 2011.

Ex-LMS Class 4 2-6-4T No.42096 in the shed yard at **Watford MPD** on March 8th, 1964.   *KCH Fairey*

The entrance to **Crystal Palace High Level station** viewed on September 20th, 1954, just before it closed.   *Marcus Eavis/Online Transport Archive*

A BR EMU arriving at **Norbiton station** on an unrecorded date in 1957.   *J Joyce/Online Transport Archive*

Printed in Malta by Melita Press

Nostalgia Rail is an imprint of Crécy Publishing Limited
1a Ringway Trading Estate
Shadowmoss Road
Manchester M22 5LH

www.crecy.co.uk

INTRODUCTION

Elmers End station and Tram Stop viewed on June 25th, 2016 *(See Map 7A).*

This "Then and Now" atlas is based on the railway system as recorded on the Railway Clearing House map of London, issued in 1921* and compares it to the lines and stations operational on January 1st, 2016. The two maps are disposed on facing pages enabling easy reference between the two.

Compared to the "Then and Now" atlas of the rest of the country† whereas the obvious difference with the latter is just how many lines have disappeared, in contrast the London area has very few closures and many additional lines have been constructed, with more to come: Crossrail 2, HS2 and Northern Line extension all in the pipeline. The "Now" map also features the modern use of the closed lines, walkways, roads etc.

The "Then" map pages are illustrated with artefacts and photographs from the 20thC and the "Now" from the 21st. Unless stated all photographs are by the authors.

The RCH map is reproduced with no amendments or corrections. Typical of the inaccuracies, regarding the publication date, are a few stations that do not qualify to be included (eg. **Camberwell** [Map 15 1C, closed April 3rd, 1916] and **Southwark Park** [Map 25 4A, closed March 15th, 1915]), however considering the original objective of the atlas, to advise of distances between major points, junctions and stations etc. it could be considered to be very practical to include them.

For clarity all tunnels have been omitted and where the terms "now" or "currently" are used in the text this refers to 2016.

Official Railway Map of London and its Environs Prepared and Published At the Railway Clearing House, London 1921
† Railway Atlas, Then and Now. Paul Smith and Keith Turner

Paul Jordan, **Walsall** and Paul Smith, Kings Heath, **Birmingham** 2016

ABBREVIATIONS

The abbreviations used in this book will be familiar to many of those whose interests lie in railways but for clarification they are reproduced thus;

BR: British Railways, **DLR:** Docklands Light Railway, **GCR:** Great Central Railway, **GER:** Great Eastern Railway, **GNR:** Great Northern Railway, **GWR:** Great Western Railway, **LB&SCR:** London, Brighton & South Coast Railway, **L&NER:** London & North Eastern Railway, **L&NWR:** London & North Western Railway, **L&SWR:** London and South Western Railway, **LC&DR:** London, Chatham & Dover Railway, **LM&SR:** London Midland & Scottish Railway, **LPTB:** London Passenger Transport Board, **LTE:** London Transport Executive, **MR:** Midland Railway, **SER:** South Eastern Railway, **SE&CR:** South Eastern & Chatham Railway, **SR:** Southern Railway, **TfL:** Transport for London

KEY TO MAP PAGES

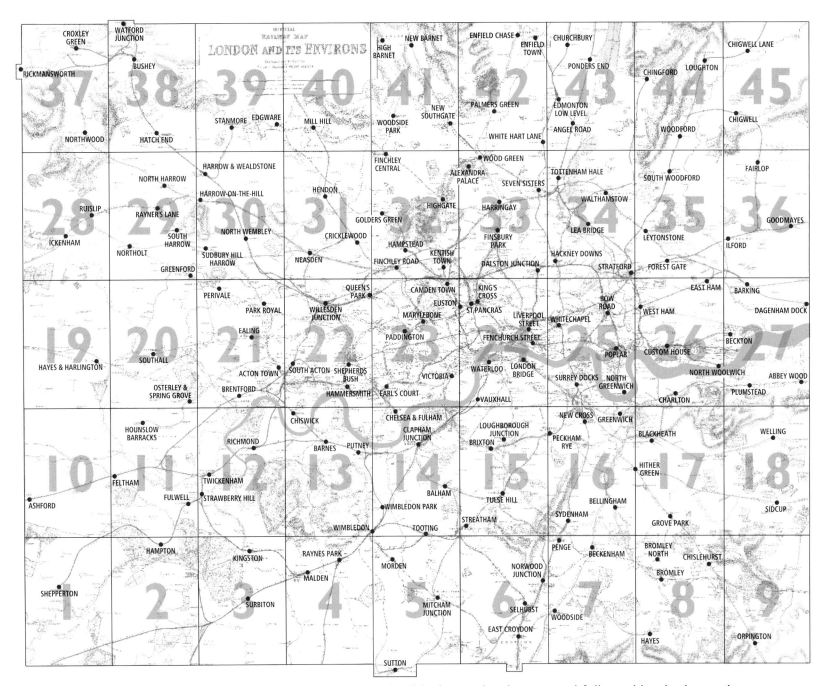

'*Then*' maps are indicated by the numeral and the '*Now*' maps by the numeral followed by the letter A.
'*Then*' and '*Now*' maps are located opposite each other for easy reference

SCALE OF MAPS

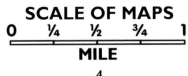

| 0 | ¼ | ½ | ¾ | 1 |

MILE

KEY - 1 JANUARY 2016 MAPS

National network (other than London Overground, but including BAA-owned lines and stations) with all passenger stations open as at January 1st, 2016 ....

MILL HILL BROADWAY

London Underground:

Bakerloo Line ....

MAIDA VALE

Central Line ....

NORTHOLT

Circle Line ....

District Line ....

TURNHAM GREEN

Hammersmith & City Line ....

PLAISTOW

Jubilee Line ....

BERMONDSEY

Metropolitan Line ....

WEST HARROW

Northern Line ....

OVAL

Piccadilly Line ....

WOOD GREEN

Victoria Line ....

SEVEN SISTERS

Waterloo & City Line ....

BANK

London Tramlink ....

CENTRALE

Docklands Light Railway ....

CYPRUS

London Overground ....

SURREY QUAYS

Freight-only branches ....

Lines and routes shared by two operators (eg Bakerloo Line and London Overground) ....

Lines and routes shared by three operators (Hammersmith & City, Circle and Metropolitan lines) ....

Other Uses:

Lines and stations on 1921 maps closed to all traffic as of January 1st, 2016 (including lines and stations opened post-1921) ....

WEMBLEY STADIUM (LNER)

Trackbeds officially designated as bridle/cycle/walkways and permissive footpaths ....

Trackbeds now roadways ....

A24

In preparation for the introduction of Crossrail 1 *(subsequently known as the "Elizabeth Line")* services in 2018 **Transport for London** took over the operation of local trains from Liverpool Street to Shenfield in May 2015 and assumed responsibility for all stations between Stratford and Shenfield.

NB The colour of the station name normally indicates which company or organisation operates that station but please note that with regard to London Underground stations, where two or more lines are served then the colour allocated to the station is purely arbitrary.

MAP 10

MAP I
1921

The entrance to **Shepperton station** viewed on January 27th, 1957. It was opened by the Thames Valley Railway on November 1st, 1864 and by 1914 it had been renamed by the L&SWR as *Shepperton for Halliford*. It was reverted to *Shepperton* by BR post 1955.
Marcus Eavis/Online Transport Archive

Sunbury station, some 2 miles and 8 chains along from *Shepperton* was also was opened by the Thames Valley Railway on November 1st, 1864.

Weybridge station was opened by the London and Southampton Railway on May 21st, 1838

Looking northeast at **Weybridge station** on April 13th, 1980.
Alan Young

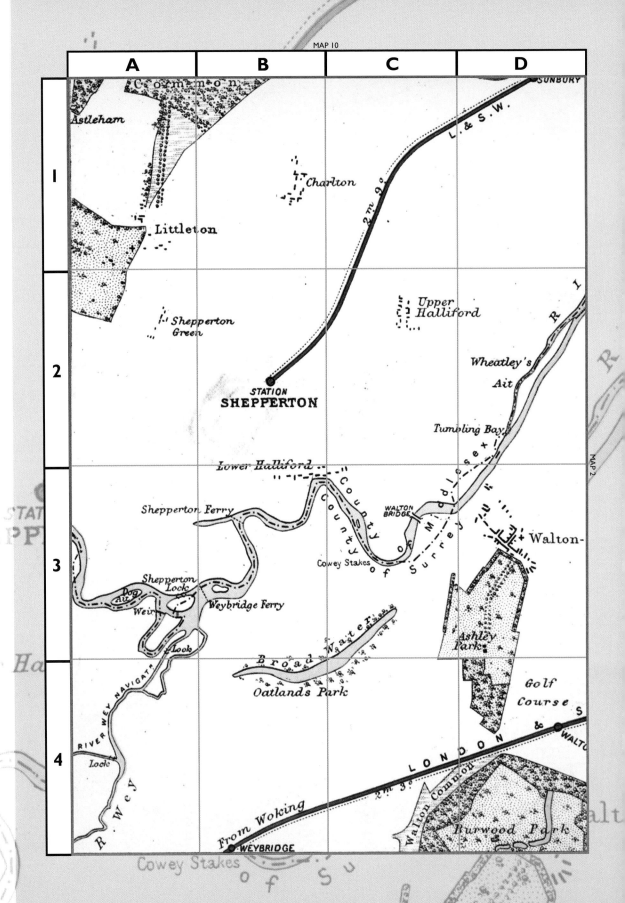

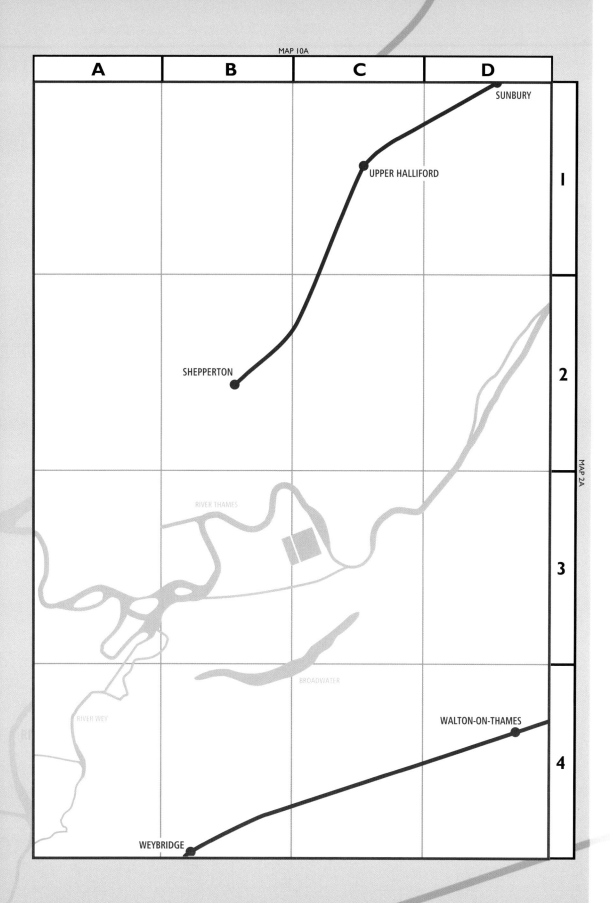

	A	B	C	D	
				SUNBURY	1
			UPPER HALLIFORD		
		SHEPPERTON			2
		RIVER THAMES			
			BROADWATER		3
	RIVER WEY			WALTON-ON-THAMES	
		WEYBRIDGE			4

Shepperton station, looking towards the buffers, on May 25th, 2016 with Class 455 EMU No.**455724** about to depart to London Waterloo.

Upper Halliford station, viewed on May 25th, 2016. It was opened by the SR on May 1st, 1944 as *Halliford Halt*, renamed twenty two days later as *Upper Halliford Halt* and as *Upper Halliford* by BR on May 5th, 1969.

Walton-on-Thames station, looking east, on May 25th, 2016. It was opened by the London & Southampton Railway on May 21st, 1838 as *Walton*, renamed as *Walton & Hersham* by the L&SWR in February 1849, as *Walton for Hersham* by 1914 and as *Walton-on-Thames* by the SR on September 30th, 1935.

It had four platforms but the two island platforms, on the up and down fast lines and visible on the right, were subsequently abandoned.

Class 458 EMU No.**458512** in the bay platform, No.1, at **Weybridge station** on May 25th, 2016.

MAP 2
1921

Hampton Court station was opened by the L&SWR on February 1st, 1849, renamed as *Hampton Court & East Moulsey* on June 1st, 1869, as *Hampton Court for Moulsey* in 1897, as *Hampton Court for East & West Molesey* in 1904, as *Hampton Court for East Molesey* in 1903 and reverted back to *Hampton Court* by BR in 1955. *Thames Ditton* is the only other station on the branch.

Claygate station viewed on May 30th, 1989.
Alan Young

Hampton Court station on January 22nd, 1977.
Alan Young

Hampton station on November 8th, 1977.
Alan Young

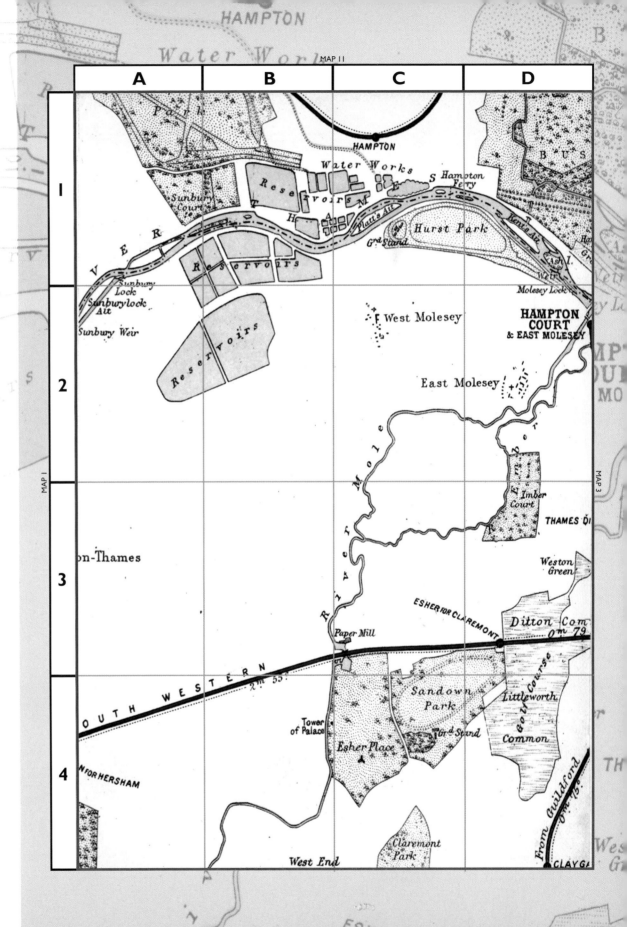

MAP 2A
January 1st, 2016

A	B	C	D

HAMPTON

1

RIVER THAMES

HAMPTON COURT

BESSBOROUGH RESERVOIR

KNIGHTS RESERVOIR

RIVER MOLE

2

QUEEN ELIZABETH II RESERVOIR

ISLAND BARN RESERVOIR

RIVER EMBER

3

ESHER

HERSHAM

4

CLAYGATE

HERSHAM

Class 455 EMU No.**455736** awaiting departure from **Hampton Court station** on May 21st, 2016.

Hampton station, looking west, on May 21st, 2016. It was opened by the Thames Valley Railway on November 1st, 1864.

Esher station, looking east, on May 25th, 2016. It was opened by the London & Southampton Railway on May 21st, 1838 as *Ditton Marsh*, renamed as *Esher & Hampton Court* by the L&SWR c1840, as *Esher & Claremont* in July 1844 and as *Esher* on June 1st, 1913.

(It has also been described as *Esher for Claremont* and *Esher for Sandown Park* in some timetables.)

Claygate station, looking north, on May 25th, 2016. It was opened by the L&SWR on February 2nd, 1885 and was known as *Claygate and Claremont* until 1913 and then *Claygate for Claremont* until 1955.

MAP 12

MAP 3
1921

BR 4-SUB EMU No.4652 arriving at **Kingston station** on an unrecorded date in 1957. The station was opened as a terminus by the L&SWR on July 1st, 1863 as *Kingston Town*. The through platforms, known as *Kingston New*, opened on January 1st, 1869 and the two stations were combined and renamed as *Kingston* on rebuilding by the SR in 1935.
J Joyce/Online Transport Archive

BR 4-SUB EMU No.4698 at **Hampton Wick station** on an unrecorded date in 1957. The station was opened by the London & South Western Railway on July 1st, 1863. *J Joyce/Online Transport Archive*

SOUTHERN RAILWAY.
(9/23)   787
TO
SURBITON

An SR-issued luggage label – destination *Surbiton!* The current **Surbiton station** was opened by the L&SWR in 1845 as *Kingston*, renamed as *Kingston Junction* in December 1852, as *Surbiton and Kingston* on July 1st, 1863 and as *Surbiton* on October 1st, 1867.

A BR EMU arriving at **Norbiton station** on an unrecorded date in 1957. The station was opened by the London & South Western Railway on January 1st, 1869. *J Joyce/Online Transport Archive*

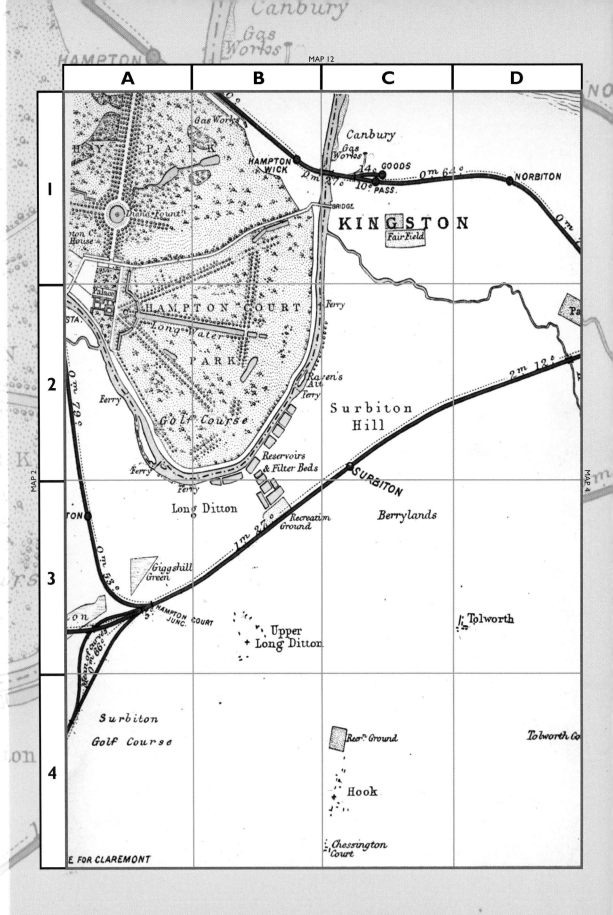

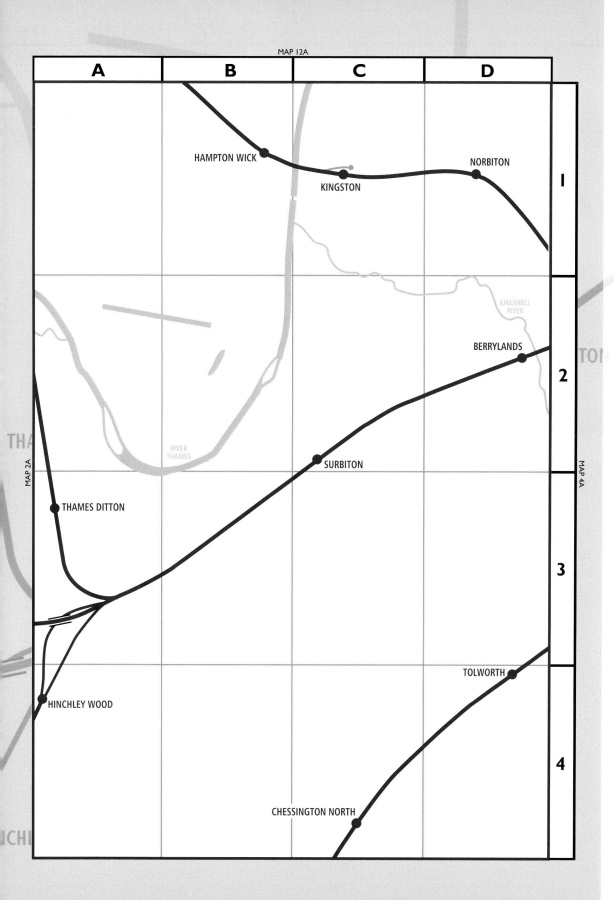

	A	B	C	D	

HAMPTON WICK

NORBITON

KINGSTON

1

KINGSMILL RIVER

BERRYLANDS

2

RIVER THAMES

SURBITON

THAMES DITTON

3

HINCHLEY WOOD

TOLWORTH

4

CHESSINGTON NORTH

MAP 3A
January 1st, 2016

Surbiton station, looking southwest, on May 21st, 2016. The station was rebuilt by the SR in *art deco* style in 1937 and is now a Grade II listed building.

Tolworth station, looking north on May 25th, 2016. It was opened by the SR on May 29th, 1938.

Hinchley Wood station was opened by the SR on October 20th, 1930 and has an unusual layout. In planform it is a "vee" with the up line passing along the west side and the down along the east. This view, taken on May 25th, 2016, shows the northbound platform in the foreground with the down, southbound, on the far side.

Norbiton station, looking west, on July 23rd, 2016.

MAP 13

MAP 4
1921

An unidentified EMU approaching **Malden station** from the west at an unknown date in 1957 – but apparently prior to the station name being changed to *New Malden*.

The station was opened by the London & South Western Railway in December 1846 and was renamed as *New Maldon & Combe* in May 1859, as *Combe and Malden* on March 1st, 1862, as *Malden for Combe* in November 1912, as *Malden* by BR in 1955 and, finally, as *New Malden* on September 16th, 1957.

J Joyce/Online Transport Archive

Malden Crossing Signal Box. Opened in 1869, the box ceased to operate as a block post on November 10th, 1974, and became an intermediate crossing-keepers cabin. The crossing gates had been replaced by lifting barriers just two months earlier and on January 30th, 1979 control of the crossing barriers was transferred to New Malden and Malden Crossing became redundant. *J Joyce/Online Transport Archive*

Raynes Park station was opened by the L&SWR on October 30th, 1871.

LEGEND
I LINE UNDER CONSTRUCTION

Wimbledon to Sutton

The Wimbledon to Sutton line had been planned in 1910 but construction was delayed by World War I. The first section, from Wimbledon to South Merton was opened by the SR on July 7th, 1929 and completed through to Sutton on January 5th, 1930.

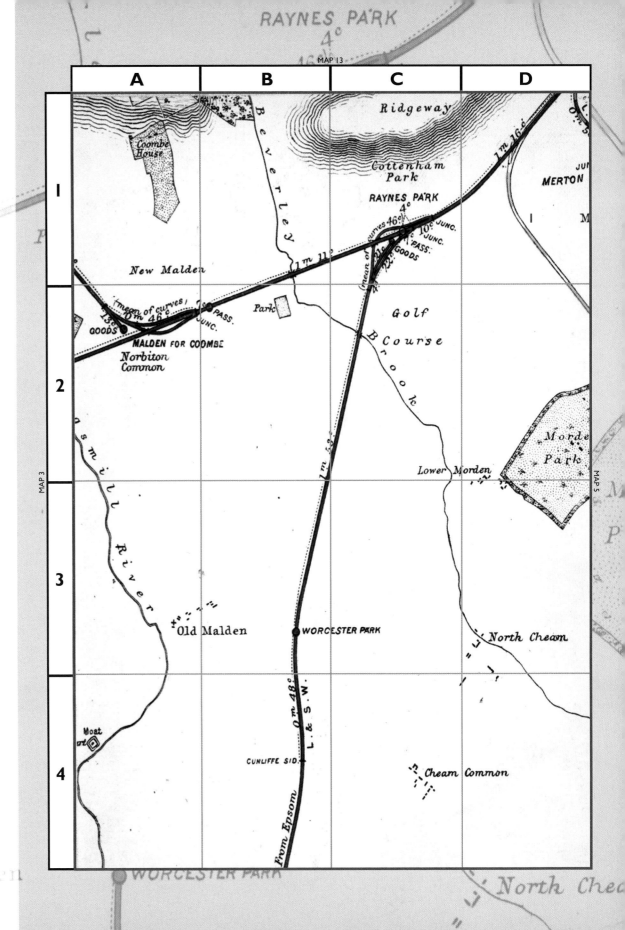

A	B	C	D

DUNDONALD ROAD

RAYNES PARK

WIMBLEDON CHASE

1

NEW MALDEN

SOUTH MERTON

BEVERLEY BROOK

2

MOTSPUR PARK

KINGSMILL RIVER

MALDEN MANOR

3

WORCESTER PARK

4

STONELEIGH

WORCESTER PARK

CR-4000 Type Tram No.2551 at **Dundonald Road Tram Stop** on March 19th, 2014. This stop, unlike others on this system, does not occupy the site of a former railway station and was opened on May 30th, 2000.

Wimbledon Chase station, looking south on July 23rd, 2016. It was opened by the SR on July 7th, 1929.

Class 455 EMU No.455729 waiting to depart from Platform No.4 at **Raynes Park station** on July 23rd, 2016.

New Malden station viewed on July 23rd, 2016. An oddity about this station is that although the island platforms are no longer used the CSI (Customer Service Information) boards are still operational.

MAP 5
1921

An EMU approaching **Merton Park station** during 1950. The station was opened by the Tooting, Merton & Wimbledon Railway on October 1st, 1868 as *Lower Merton* and renamed as *Merton Park* by the LB&SCR on September 1st, 1887. It was closed on May 31st, 1997 and subsequently demolished when the line was taken over for Route 3 of the London Tramlink. The *Merton Park Tramstop*, which opened in 2000 is partially constructed on the station site.

J Joyce/Online Transport Archive

Ex-SECR Class H 0-6-0T No.31251 at the head of *"The South Londoner"* on the Merton Abbey line in 1958.

J Joyce/Online Transport Archive

Merton Abbey station viewed in 1950, some twenty one years after it was closed by the SR.

J Joyce/Online Transport Archive

LEGEND
| LINE UNDER CONSTRUCTION

Wimbledon to Sutton

The Wimbledon to Sutton line had been planned in 1910 but construction was delayed by World War 1. The first section, from Wimbledon to South Merton was opened by the SR on July 7th, 1929 and completed through to Sutton on January 5th, 1930.

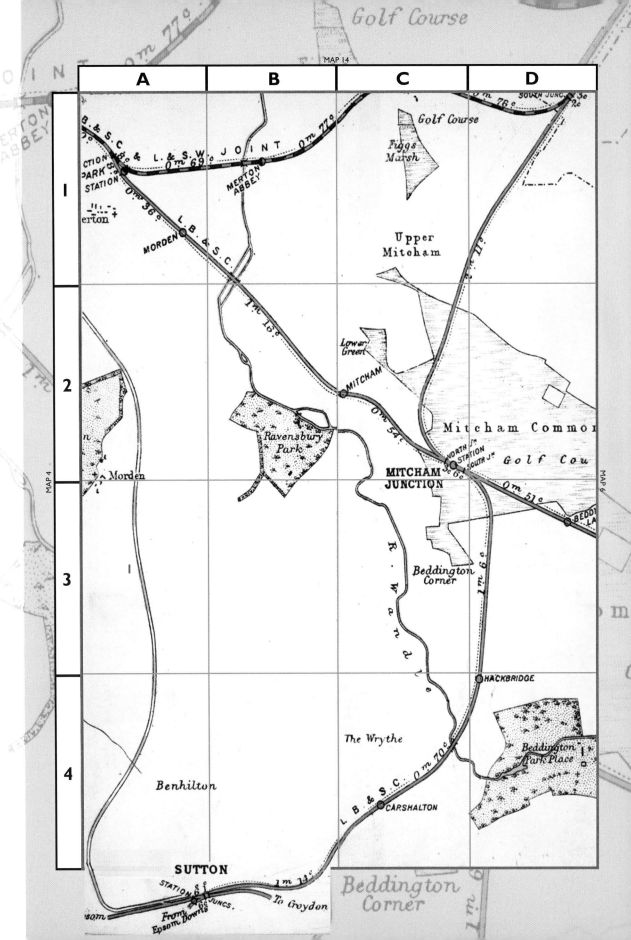

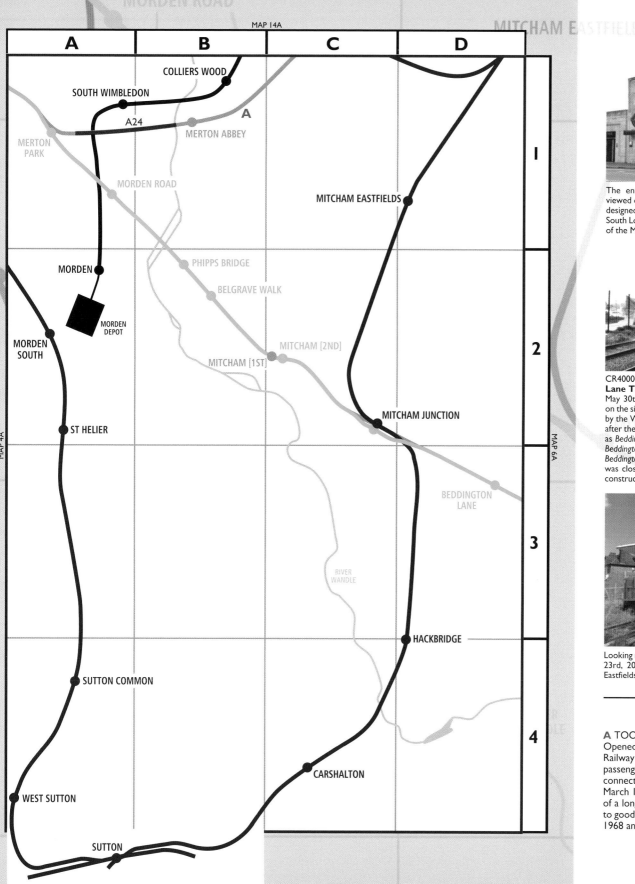

MORDEN ROAD

MITCHAM EASTFIELDS

MAP 14A

A	B	C	D

COLLIERS WOOD

SOUTH WIMBLEDON

A24

A

MERTON ABBEY

MERTON PARK

MORDEN ROAD

MITCHAM EASTFIELDS

1

PHIPPS BRIDGE

MORDEN

BELGRAVE WALK

MORDEN DEPOT

MORDEN SOUTH

MITCHAM [2ND]

MITCHAM [1ST]

MITCHAM JUNCTION

2

ST HELIER

BEDDINGTON LANE

3

RIVER WANDLE

SUTTON COMMON

HACKBRIDGE

WEST SUTTON

CARSHALTON

4

SUTTON

MAP 4A

MAP 6A

DEN TH

The entrance to **Colliers Wood tube station**, viewed on June 25th, 2016. Now Grade II listed, it was designed by Charles Holden and opened by the City & South London Railway on September 13th, 1926 as part of the Morden extension.

CR4000-type tram No.2531 approaching **Beddington Lane Tram Stop** on August 19th, 2014. Opened on May 30th, 2000 by Tramlink, the stop is constructed on the site of *Beddington Lane* station which was opened by the Wimbledon and Croydon Railway as *Beddington* after the line opened on October 22nd, 1855, renamed as *Beddington Lane* by the LB&SCR in January 1887, as *Beddington Lane Halt* in 1919 and reverted back to *Beddington Lane* by BR on May 5th, 1969. The station was closed by Railtrack on June 2nd, 1997 to enable construction of the tram stop and tramway.

Looking north at **Mitcham Eastfields station** on July 23rd, 2016. It has staggered platforms, each side of Eastfields Road, and was opened on June 2nd, 2008.

LEGEND
CLOSED LINES
A TOOTING JUNCTION – MERTON PARK
Opened by the Tooting, Merton & Wimbledon Railway on October 1st, 1868 and closed to passengers by the SR on March 3rd, 1929. The connection at Tooting Junction was severed on March 10th, 1934 and the line assumed the role of a long siding from Merton Park. BR closed it to goods north of Merton Park from August 5th, 1968 and totally on May 5th, 1975.

MAP 6
1921

Addiscombe station on March 12th, 1988 with the EMU depot visible on the left.

The station was opened by the Mid-Kent Railway on April 1st, 1864 as *Croydon (Addiscombe Road)* and renamed as *Croydon (Addiscombe)* by the SR on April 1st, 1925, as *Addiscombe (Croydon)* on February 28th, 1926, and as *Addiscombe* by BR on June 13th, 1955.

The signal box, on the right in the picture, burned down in March 1996 and the adjacent EMU shed which had opened on July 11th, 1925 was dispensed with in October 1992. The station closed on May 31st, 1997 and remained derelict until demolition in 2001. A housing estate now occupies the site. *Phil Mackie*

The remains of the street level entrance to **Bingham Road station** viewed on March 12th, 1988.

It was opened by the SR on September 30th, 1935 and replaced an earlier station that had been opened by the Woodside & Croydon Joint Railway as *Bingham Road Halt* on September 1st, 1906 and closed on March 13th, 1915. *Bingham Road* station was closed by BR on May 15th, 1983 and subsequently demolished to make way for the London Tramlink which commenced operating along the route on May 10th, 2000.

The station was used for a scene in the 1961 Tony Hancock film "The Rebel". *Phil Mackie*

Norwood Junction MPD viewed in BR days. It was opened by the SR in 1935 and closed by BR on June 5th, 1964.

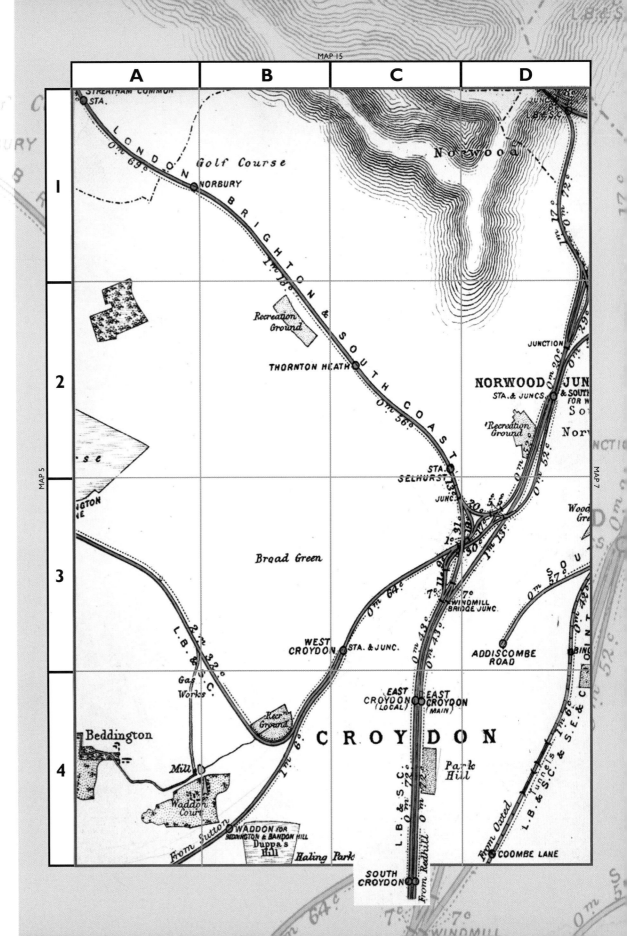

MAP 6A
January 1st, 2016

	A	B	C	D	
	STREATHAM COMMON			CRYSTAL PALACE	1
	NORBURY				
			THORNTON HEATH		2
				NORWOOD JUNCTION	
			SELHURST	SELHURST DEPOT	
	THERAPIA LANE			BLACKHORSE LANE	3
	THERAPIA LANE DEPOT			A	
	AMPERE WAY			ADDISCOMBE ROAD ADDISCOMBE	
		WEST CROYDON	WELLESLEY ROAD	BINGHAM ROAD	
	WADDON MARSH [1ST]				
	WADDON MARSH [2ND]	AMPERE	EAST CROYDON	SANDILANDS	
				LEBANON ROAD	4
	WANDLE PARK	REEVES CORNER CHURCH STREET GEORGE STREET			
	WADDON			COOMBE LANE B	
			SOUTH CROYDON		

Class 378 EMU No.**378142** at **Crystal Palace station** on March 19th, 2014. The station was opened by the West End of London & Crystal Palace Railway on June 10th, 1854 to convey passengers to The Crystal Palace and was worked from the outset by the LB&SCR.

Following the arrival of the *Crystal Palace High Level* station in 1854 *(See note on Map 15)* it was renamed as *Crystal Palace Low Level* by the SR during 1933/34 and reverted back to *Crystal Palace* by BR on June 13th, 1955.

Looking south at **Waddon station** on May 25th, 2016. The station was opened by the LB&SCR in February 1863.

Looking south at **West Croydon station** on July 23rd, 2016. It was opened by the L&SWR on June 5th, 1839 as *Croydon* and renamed as *West Croydon* in April 1851.

LEGEND
CLOSED LINES
A ADDISCOMBE ROAD BRANCH
The line was opened to *Addiscombe Road (Croydon)* station by the Mid-Kent Railway on April 1st, 1864 and closed on June 2nd, 1997.

The section between East India Way and the *Blackhorse Lane Tram Stop* is now the Addiscombe Linear Park.
B COOMBE LANE – SELSDON
This short link line was opened by the SER and the LB&SCR on August 10th, 1885 and closed by BR on May 16th, 1983.

MAP 7
1921

Elmers End station viewed on March 12th, 1988. It was opened by the South Eastern Railway on April 1st, 1864 and Platform No.1 became a terminus for one of the London Tramlink routes on May 29th, 2000.
Phil Mackie

Anerley station viewed on May 29th, 1974. It was opened by the London & Croydon Railway on June 5th, 1839 as *Anerley Bridge* and renamed as *Anerley* by the LB&SCR in 1840.
Alan Young

Clock House station on June 14th, 1975. It was opened by the SER on May 1st, 1890.
Alan Young

Looking west at **Eden Park station** on February 3rd, 1979. It was opened by the SER (West Wickham & Hayes Railway) on May 29th, 1882.
Alan Young

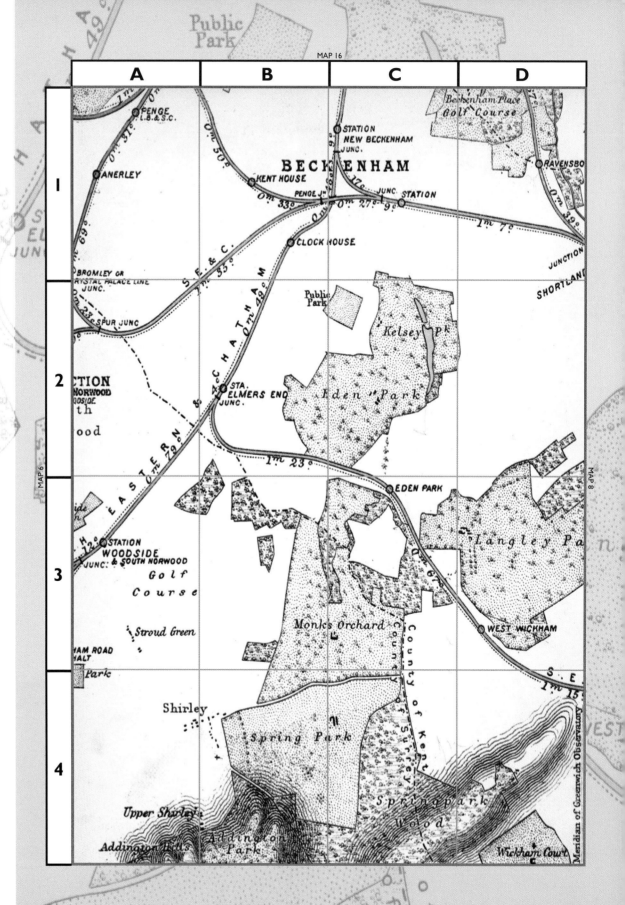

BECKENHAM ROAD

MAP 16A

	A	B	C	D	

PENGE WEST

ANERLEY

NEW BECKENHAM

RAVENSBOURNE

KENT HOUSE

BECKENHAM ROAD

BECKENHAM JUNCTION

1

CLOCK HOUSE

AVENUE ROAD

BIRKBECK

HARRINGTON ROAD

ELMERS END

2

ARENA

EDEN PARK

A WOODSIDE

3

WEST WICKHAM

4

MAP 6A

MAP 8A

Variobahn-type tram No.**2559** at **Arena tram stop** on June 25th, 2016. The line, from *Elmers End* to *Addiscombe* was opened by the Mid-Kent Railway on April 1st, 1864 and closed on June 2nd, 1997 for conversion to Tramlink. *Arena Tram Stop* opened, along with the tramway, on May 30th, 2000.

Birkbeck station, looking east on June 25th, 2016. The line was opened by the West End of London & Crystal Palace Railway on May 3rd, 1858 but the station was not opened until March 2nd, 1930 by the SR. The line was singled by BR in February 1983 and the former "up" (Westbound) line converted to Tramlink, reopening on May 23rd, 2000.
  Birkbeck tram stop, which opened on the same day, can be seen on the right.

Looking east at **Beckenham Junction station** on June 25th, 2016. The station was opened by the Mid-Kent Railway on January 1st 1857 as *Beckenham* and renamed as *Beckenham Junction* by the SE&CR on April 1st, 1864.

LEGEND
CLOSED LINE
A ADDISCOMBE ROAD BRANCH
The line was opened to *Addiscombe Road (Croydon) station* by the Mid-Kent Railway on April 1st, 1864 and closed on June 2nd, 1997.

MAP 8
1921

MAP 17

BR 4-EPB EMU No.5182 standing in **Bromley North station** on February 12th, 1987. The station was opened by the Bromley Direct Railway on January 1st, 1878 as *Bromley* and renamed as *Bromley North* by the South Eastern Railway on July 1st, 1899.   *Phil Mackie*

A 4-car ex-Brighton set leaves **Shortlands station** on an unknown date. The station was opened by the West End of London & Crystal Palace (Farnborough Extension) Railway on May 3rd, 1858 as *Bromley* and renamed as *Shortlands* on July 1st, 1858.
Marcus Eavis/Online Transport Archive

Hayes station on March 12th, 1988. It was opened by the West Wickham & Hayes Railway on May 29th, 1882 as *Hayes* and renamed by BR as *Hayes (Kent)* after 1964. *Hayes for Keston* was used in Bradshaw between 1913 and 1955.   *Phil Mackie*

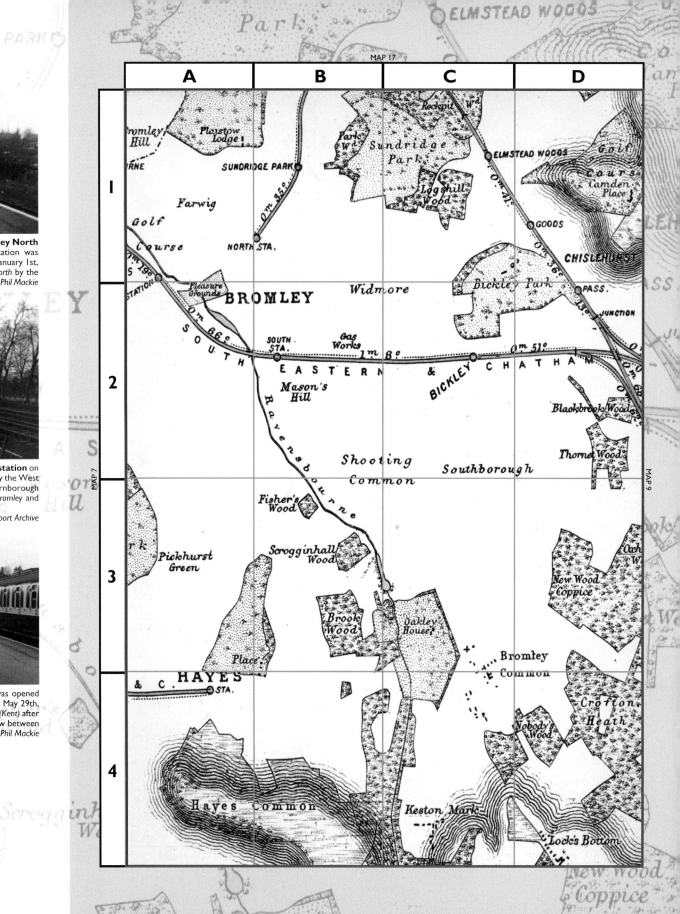

A   B   C   D

ELMSTEAD WOODS

SUNDRIDGE PARK

1

BROMLEY NORTH

SHORTLANDS

CHISELHURST

BROMLEY SOUTH

BICKLEY

2

RAVENSBOURNE

3

HAYES

4

Looking north at **Sundridge Park station** on June 25th, 2016. It was opened by the Bromley Direct Railway on January 1st, 1878 as *Plaistow* and renamed as *Sundridge Park* by the South Eastern Railway on July 1st, 1894.

Hayes station, viewed on June 25th, 2016.

Bickley station, viewed from the west on June 25th, 2016. As originally opened by the Mid-Kent Railway on July 5th, 1858 and named *Southborough Road* it was the terminus of the line from *Bromley*. It became a through station when linked up with LC&DR metals from the east and was renamed as *Bickley* by the SER on October 1st, 1860.

Bromley North station on June 25th, 2016.

MAP 9
1921

Orpington station viewed on September 26th, 1987. The station was opened by the South Eastern Railway on March 2nd, 1868 and enlarged in 1904. The EMU stabling sidings were removed in the 1990s to accommodate further station expansion. *Phil Mackie*

A BR-issued platform ticket for **Orpington station**

Looking north from **Orpington station** on September 26th, 1987 towards Orpington EMU Depot which was opened by the SR in 1935 and closed by BR on May 10th, 1992.

The former steam shed which was opened by the SE&CR in 1901 and closed by the SR in 1925 is still extant on the east side of the station at the north end, having been used by the Permanent Way Department and latterly as a Driver Training Centre. *Phil Mackie*

A BR-issued platform ticket for **St Mary Cray station**

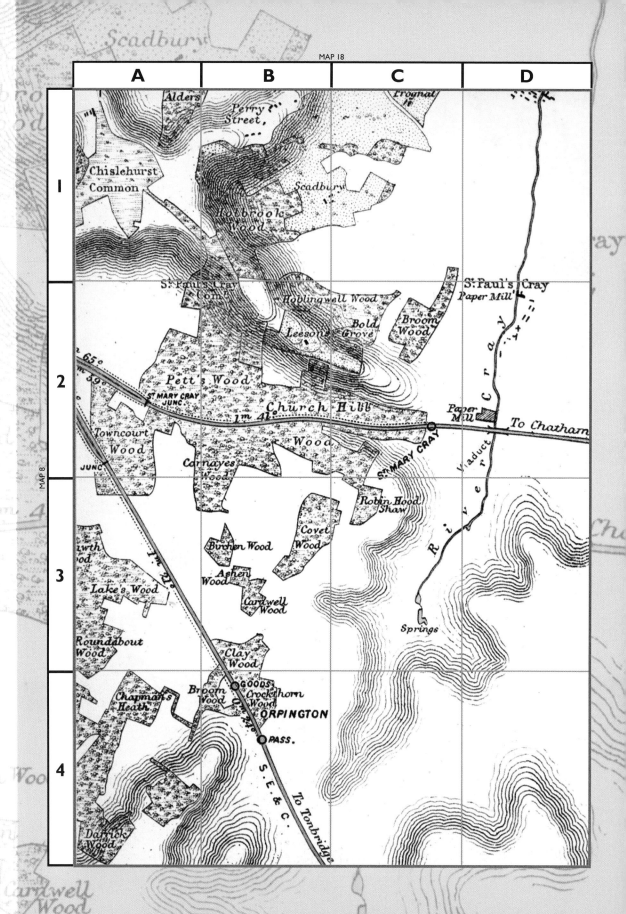

A	B	C	D

1

2

RIVER
CRAY

ST MARY CRAY

PETTS WOOD

3

ORPINGTON

4

ORPINGTON

Petts Wood station, looking north, on May 25th, 2016. It was opened by the SR on July 9th, 1928.

Looking west along Platform No.2 at **St Mary Cray station** on May 25th, 2016 with Class 465 EMU No.465912 about to depart. The station was opened by the London, Chatham & Dover Railway on December 3rd, 1860.

Orpington station, looking southeast, on June 25th, 2016 with Class 425 EMU No.465238 standing at Platform No.6.

MAP 10
1921

Ashford station was opened by the Windsor, Staines & South West Railway on August 22nd, 1848 and renamed as *Ashford (Middlesex)* by the SR on July 9th, 1923 to distinguish it from the other Ashford station on their system; *Ashford (Kent)*. It was renamed as *Ashford* by BR on June 12th, 1961, as *Ashford (Surrey)* on May 12th, 1980, as *Ashford (Middlesex)* on May 24th, 1998 and subsequently as *Ashford (Surrey)*.

Ashford station viewed from a passing train on June 1st, 1986.
Alan Young

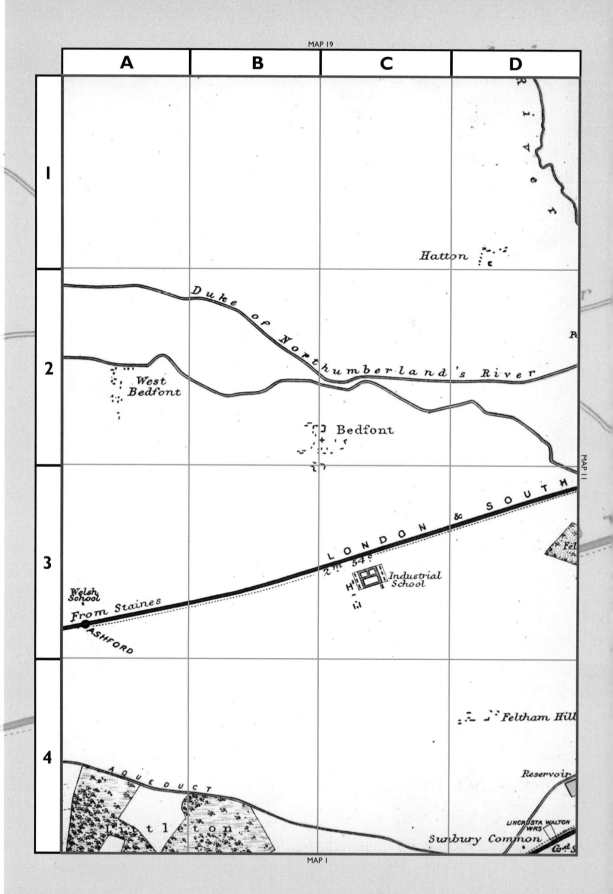

MAP 19A

A	B	C	D

SEE INSET

A

RIVER CRANE

1

HEATHROW
TERMINALS
2 & 3

HATTON CROSS

LONDON
HEATHROW
AIRPORT

DUKE OF NORTHUMBERLAND'S RIVER

HEATHROW
TERMINAL 4

LONGFORD
RIVER

2

MAP 11A

3

ASHFORD

HEATHROW
TERMINAL 5

4

MAP 1A

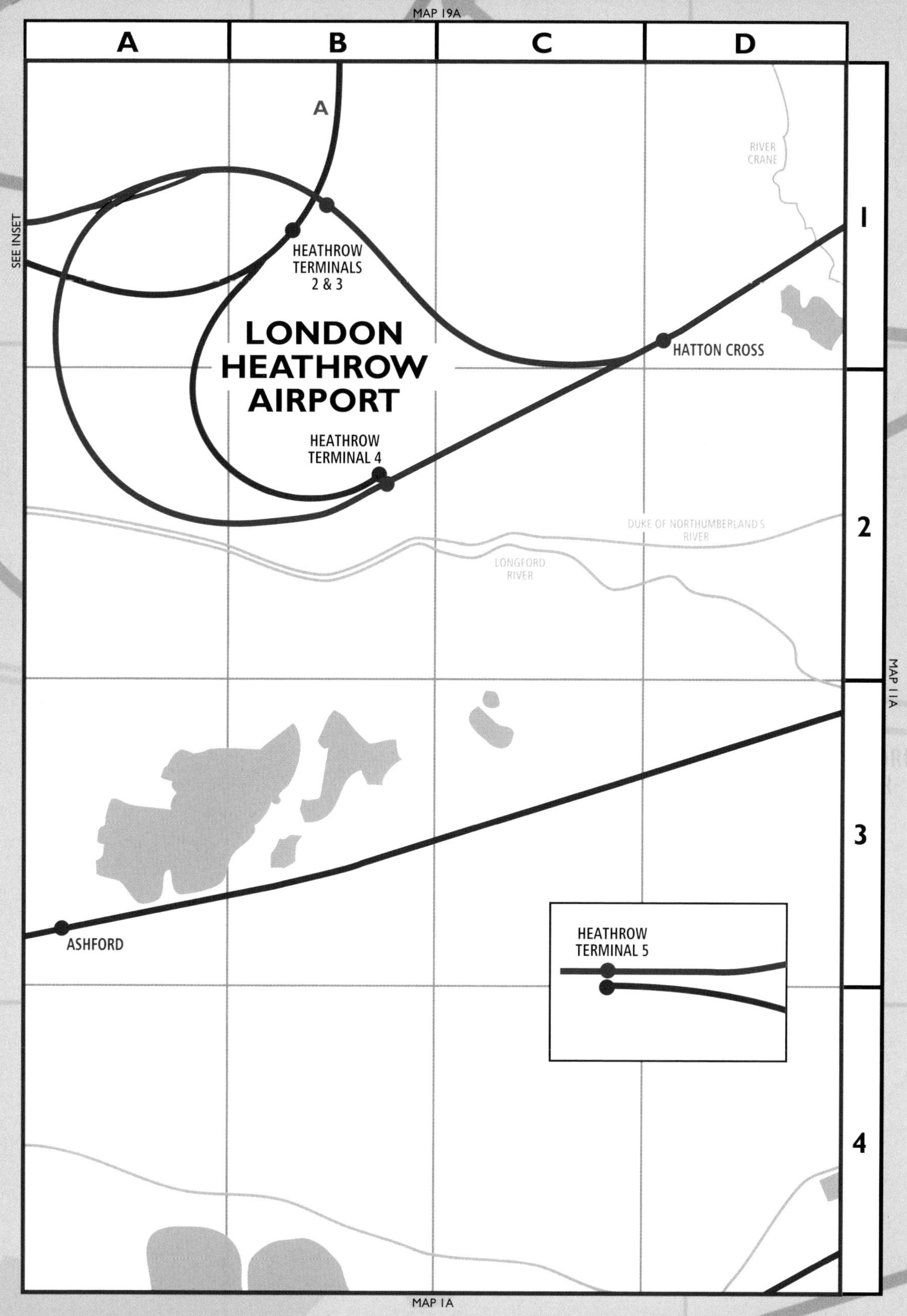

Ashford station, looking west, on May 25th, 2016 with Class 458 EMU No.**458502** about to depart on a service to London Waterloo.

The entrance to **Hatton Cross Tube station** viewed on July 17th, 2016. When opened on July 19th, 1975 it was the terminus of the first phase of the Piccadilly Line extension from *Hounslow West* and became a "through" station on December 16th, 1977 with completion of the line to *Heathrow Central* (Now *Heathrow Terminals 2 and 3*).

LEGEND

A The line and stations beyond the Boundary Point are the property of Heathrow Airport Holdings.

The Heathrow Express stations at *Heathrow Terminals 1, 2 & 3* and *Heathrow Terminal 4* both opened on May 25th, 1998 when the temporary station at *Heathrow Junction* – opened on January 19th, 1998 – closed for the second time (the service was suspended between January 31st and February 3rd, 1998 due to wheel damage).

Heathrow Terminals 1, 2 & 3 station was renamed as *Heathrow Central* and subsequently *Heathrow Terminals 2 & 3*

The joint Heathrow Express/LUL station at *Heathrow Terminal 5* opened on March 27th, 2008.

MAP 20

MAP 11
1921

A large marshalling yard was built on the south side of the line and east of Feltham station. Construction was commenced by the L&SWR prior to grouping and was eventually completed by the SR. **Feltham MPD** was opened by the L&SWR in 1922 to service engines working and visiting the yard and was closed by BR at the end of steam on the Southern Region on July 9th, 1967. Prior to the depot's closure a small diesel depot was built west of the shed but this appears to have had very little use, closing in c1969 when the yard was dispensed with. The depot was photographed on September 25th, 1963.
WT Stubbs

BR EMU No.1851 at the west end of **Feltham station** on an unknown date. The station was opened by the Windsor, Staines & South Western Railway on August 22nd, 1848.
Marcus Eavis/Online Transport Archive

Looking west at **Fulwell for Hampton Hill station** on November 8th, 1975. It was opened by the Thames Valley Railway on November 1st, 1864 as *Fulwell*, renamed as *Fulwell (New Hampton)* by the L&SWR in 1874, as *Fulwell for Hampton Hill* in 1887 and reverted back to *Fulwell* by BR.
Alan Young

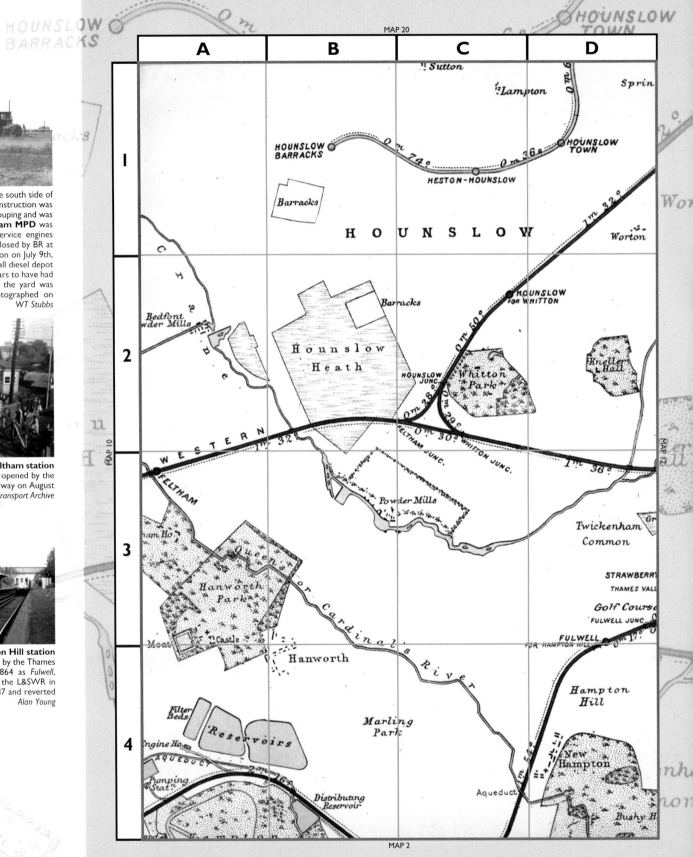

MAP 2

A | B | C | D

HOUNSLOW
WEST

HOUNSLOW
BARRACKS

HOUNSLOW
EAST

HOUNSLOW
CENTRAL

1

HOUNSLOW

2

WHITTON

FELTHAM

RIVER
CRANE

3

FULWELL

LONGFORD
RIVER

4

KEMPTON PARK

MAP 20A

MAP 10A

MAP 2A

Kempton Park station, looking west, on May 25th, 2016 with Class 455 EMU No.**455710** at Platform No.2 on a westbound service . It was opened by the L&SWR on July 18th, 1878 and until March 6th, 2006 was only used for events at the adjacent racecourse. It now has regular services.

Feltham station, looking west, on July 17th, 2016.

Class 458 EMU No.**458516** at **Whitton station** on July 17th, 2016. It was opened by the SR on July 6th, 1930.

The entrance to **Hounslow West tube station** viewed on July 17th, 2016. It was opened by the LTE on July 14th, 1975 when the Piccadilly Line was extended to *Hatton Cross*. The previous station, which had been opened by the District Railway on July 21st, 1884 as *Hounslow Barracks*, was not on a suitable alignment for the extension.

MAP 12
1921

North Sheen station was opened on July 6th, 1930 by the SR.

Teddington station viewed on June 25th, 1986. It was opened by the L&SWR on July 1st 1863 as *Teddington (Bushey Park)*, renamed as *Teddington & Bushey Park* in July 1908, as *Teddington for Bushey Park* in August 1911 and renamed as *Teddington* by BR.
Alan Young

Despite being of LM&SR origin and 3rd class, this ticket was issued on August 17th, 1967 and is an extreme example of the practice of utilizing rarely-used old stock!

Strawberry Hill station on November 8th, 1975. It was opened by the L&SWR on December 1st, 1873.
Alan Young

	A	**B**	**C**	**D**	

SYON LANE

A

ISLEWORTH

KEW GARDENS

DUKE OF NORTHUMBERLAND'S RIVER

1

RIVER THAMES

RICHMOND

NORTH SHEEN

RICHMOND BRIDGE

RIVER CRANE

ST MARGARETS

2

TWICKENHAM [2ND]

TWICKENHAM [1ST]

STRAWBERRY HILL

STRAWBERRY HILL DEPOT

3

TEDDINGTON

4

MAP 12A
January 1st, 2016

Looking south at **Kew Gardens station** on May 21st, 2016. It was opened by the L&SWR on January 1st, 1869 and the station, including the footbridge, is Grade II listed. The District Railway *(later London Underground District Line)* started operating services here on June 1st, 1877 and today the station is shared with London Overground.

Looking west along the through platforms at **Richmond station** on May 21st, 2016 with the bay platforms partially visible on the right.

The through line station was opened by the Windsor Staines & South Western Railway on August 22nd, 1848 and a five-platform terminus was opened on the north side by the L&SWR on January 1st, 1869. The two stations were rebuilt and combined by the SR and opened on August 1st, 1937. The bay platforms are currently used by London Overground and the District Line and South West Trains operates through services.

Looking west at **Twickenham station** on May 21st, 2016. The station was opened by BR on March 28th, 1954 and replaced one sited some 250 yards to the west and opened by the Windsor Staines & South Western Railway on August 22nd, 1848.

LEGEND

A BRENTFORD BRANCH
Opened by the GWR on July 18th, 1859 and closed to passengers on May 4th, 1942, the line was lifted beyond Brentford Goods and is currently used to serve an aggregate depot and refuse transfer station.

MAP 13
1921

Ex-SE&CR Class 0395 0-6-0 No.30567 entering **Wimbledon station** on an enthusiasts' special at some time during the 1950s.
Joyce/Online Transport Archive

Barnes Bridge station in April 1971. It was opened by the L&SWR on March 12th, 1916.
Graham Larkbey

Looking west at **Putney station** on May 27th, 1974. It was opened by the Richmond & West End Railway on July 27th, 1846. *Alan Young*

Mortlake station in 1971. It was opened by the Richmond & West End Railway on July 22nd, 1846, renamed as *Mortlake & East Sheen* by the L&SWR on April 1st, 1886, as *Mortlake for East Sheen* in 1916 and reverted back to *Mortlake* by BR in 1955.
Graham Larkbey

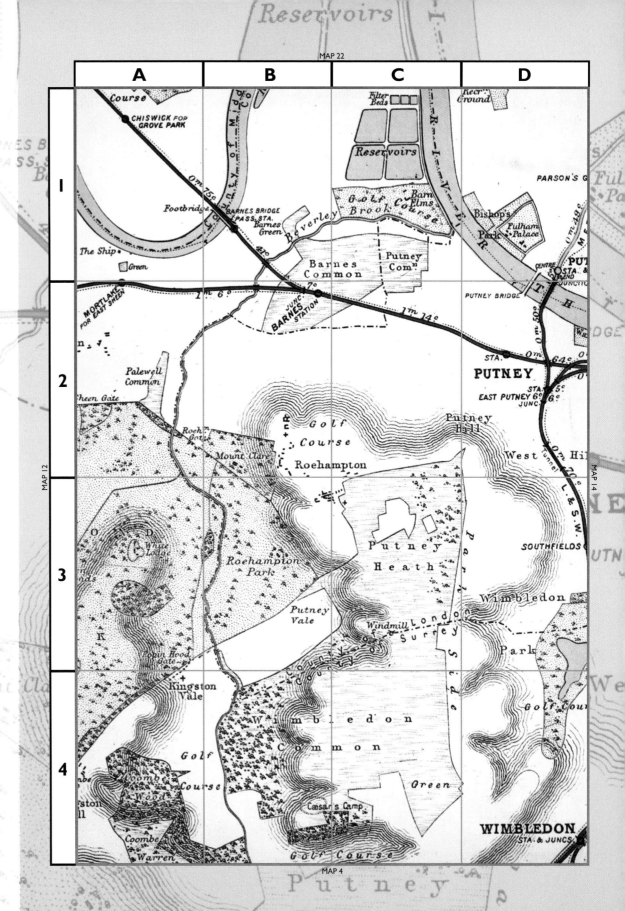

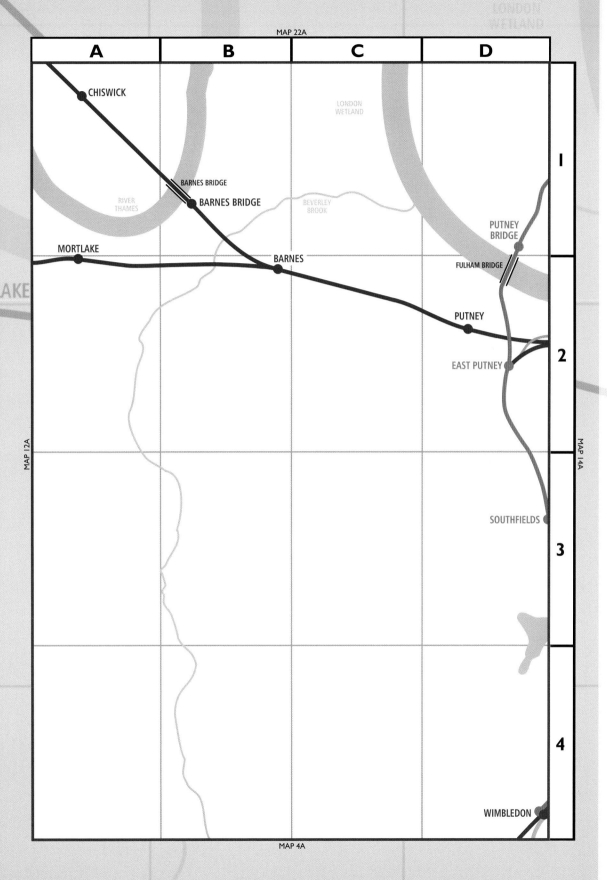

MAP 22A

A	B	C	D

CHISWICK

1

BARNES BRIDGE

BARNES BRIDGE

RIVER THAMES

BEVERLEY BROOK

LONDON WETLAND

PUTNEY BRIDGE

MORTLAKE

BARNES

FULHAM BRIDGE

2

PUTNEY

EAST PUTNEY

MAP 12A

MAP 14A

SOUTHFIELDS

3

4

WIMBLEDON

MAP 4A

Looking west at **Barnes station** on May 21st, 2016. Now Grade II listed, It was opened by the Richmond & West End Railway on July 27th, 1846.

Looking west at **Wimbledon station** on May 21st, 2016. It was opened by the L&SWR on November 21st, 1881 as *Wimbledon & Merton*, replacing the original station which had been opened by the London & Southampton Railway on May 21st,1838 and sited on the west side of the road bridge.

The District Railway established a terminus for its line from *Putney Bridge* on the north side of the station on June 3rd, 1889 and it was renamed as *Wimbledon* on June 1st, 1909. The station was rebuilt by the SR in the 1920s and since May 30th, 2000 has been the western terminus of the London Tramlink.

An S7 Stock train, with car No.21314 leading, at **Putney Bridge tube station** on July 26th, 2014. The station was opened by the District Railway on March 1st, 1880 as *Putney Bridge & Fulham* and was a terminus until June 3rd, 1889 when the bridge was completed and the line extended to Wimbledon. It was renamed as *Putney Bridge & Hurlingham* on January 1st, 1902 and as *Putney Bridge* in 1938/39.

Class 458 EMU No.458527 at **Putney station** on May 21st, 2016. It was opened by the Richmond & West End Railway on July 27th,1846 and extensively rebuilt when the line was quadrupled in 1886.

MAP 14
1921

A 1950 view of **Haydons Road station**. It was opened by the Tooting, Merton & Wimbledon Railway on October 1st, 1868 as *Haydens Lane* and renamed as *Haydons Road* on October 1st, 1889. The station was closed on January 1st, 1917 and reopened by the SR on August 27th, 1923. *J Joyce/Online Transport Archive*

Looking east in 1950 at the remains of the first **Tooting station** which was opened by the Tooting, Merton & Wimbledon Railway on October 1st, 1868 and closed and replaced by a second *Tooting* station more conveniently sited some 300 yards to the east on August 12th, 1894. The new station, which was renamed as *Tooting Junction* in 1904 and closed on January 1st 1917, was reopened by the SR on August 27th, 1923 and renamed as *Tooting* on March 1st, 1938,

After closure the original station building, which can be seen on the left, was used as a private residence until 2004 when it was demolished and a small housing estate constructed on the site. Fragments of the platforms still survive today. *J Joyce/Online Transport Archive*

Wandsworth Town station viewed on October 14th, 1978. It was opened by the Richmond & West End Railway on July 27th, 1846 as *Wandsworth* and renamed as *Wandsworth Town* by the L&SWR on October 7th, 1903. *Alan Young*

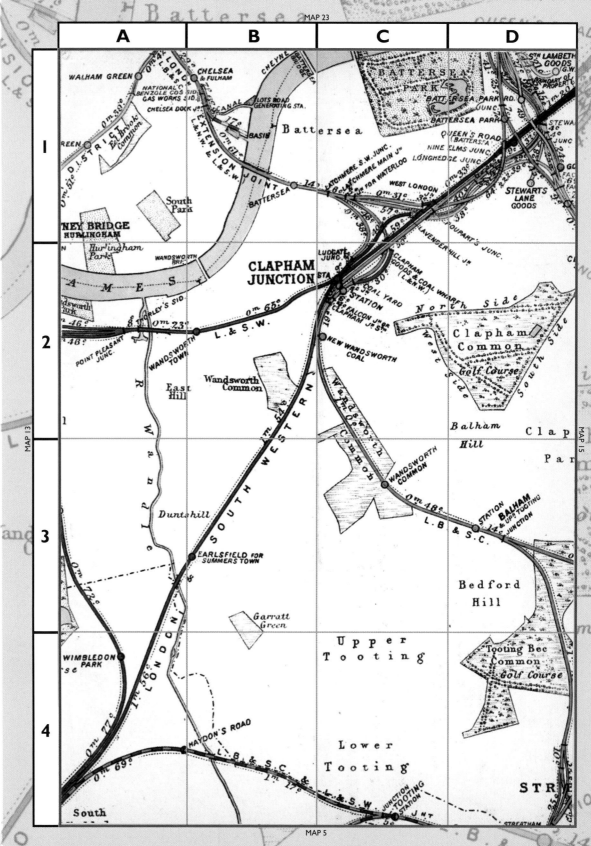

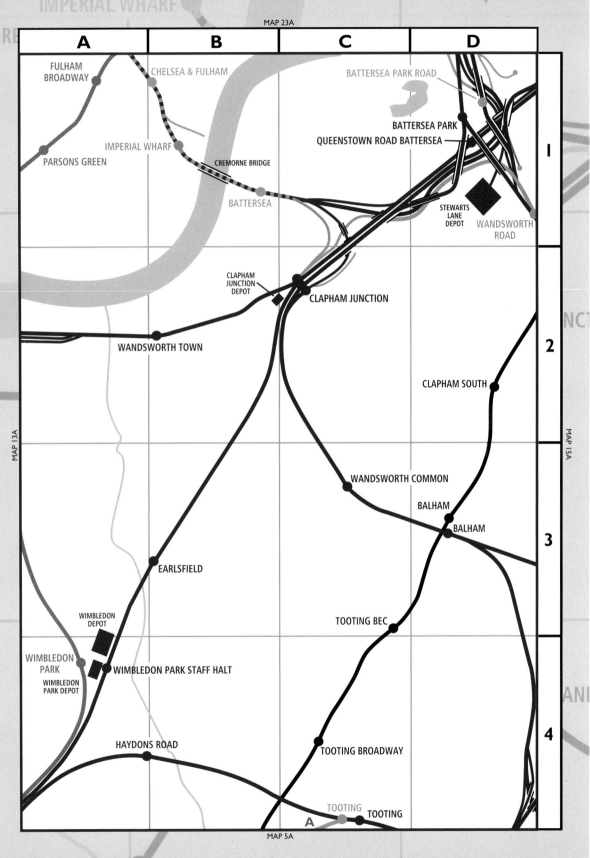

MAP 23A

| A | B | C | D |

FULHAM BROADWAY

CHELSEA & FULHAM

BATTERSEA PARK ROAD

IMPERIAL WHARF

PARSONS GREEN

CREMORNE BRIDGE

BATTERSEA PARK

QUEENSTOWN ROAD BATTERSEA

BATTERSEA

STEWARTS LANE DEPOT

WANDSWORTH ROAD

1

CLAPHAM JUNCTION DEPOT

CLAPHAM JUNCTION

WANDSWORTH TOWN

2

CLAPHAM SOUTH

WANDSWORTH COMMON

BALHAM
BALHAM

3

EARLSFIELD

TOOTING BEC

WIMBLEDON DEPOT

WIMBLEDON PARK

WIMBLEDON PARK STAFF HALT

WIMBLEDON PARK DEPOT

HAYDONS ROAD

TOOTING BROADWAY

4

TOOTING
TOOTING

A

MAP 5A

MAP 13A

MAP 15A

Battersea Park station, viewed on May 21st, 2016. with the Clapham Junction platforms in the foreground and the Brixton line diverging to the left. It was opened by the LB&SCR on May 1st, 1867 as *York Road*, renamed as *York Road & Battersea Park* on November 1st, 1870, as *Battersea Park & York Road* on January 1st, 1877 and as *Battersea Park* on June 1st, 1885.

Platform No.1 (on the Brixton line) is disused and the line has been lifted.

Looking south at **Parsons Green tube station** on March 8th, 2014 with C stock car No.**5549** trailing on a service to *Wimbledon*. The station was opened by the District Railway on March 1st, 1880.

Looking east at **Wandsworth Town station** on May 21st, 2016. It was opened by the Richmond & West End Railway on July 27th, 1846 as *Wandsworth* and renamed as *Wandsworth Town* by the L&SWR on October 7th, 1903.

LEGEND
CLOSED LINES
A TOOTING JUNCTION – MERTON PARK
Opened by the Tooting, Merton & Wimbledon Railway on October 1st, 1868 and closed to passengers by the SR on March 3rd, 1929. The connection at Tooting Junction was severed on March 10th, 1934 and the line assumed the role of a long siding from Merton Park. BR closed it to goods north of Merton Park from August 5th, 1968 and totally on May 5th, 1975.

MAP 15
1921

East Brixton station viewed on March 18th, 1956. It was opened by the LB&SCR on August 13th, 1856 as *Loughborough Park*, renamed as *Loughborough Park & Brixton* on January 1st, 1870 and as *East Brixton* on January 1st, 1894. The station was closed by the SR on May 19th, 1926, reopened on September 20th, 1926 and finally closed by BR on January 5th, 1976. It was subsequently demolished.

Marcus Eavis/Online Transport Archive

BR Class 415/4 4-EPB EMU No.5435 at **Streatham Hill station** on November 12th, 1998. Streatham Hill EMU Depot can be seen on the left. *Phil Mackie*

Despite the "Southern Electric" nomenclature this view of the entrance to **Crystal Palace High Level station** was taken just before it closed on September 20th, 1954. A BR poster can be seen inside the entrance giving advance warning of the proposed closure!

It was opened on August 1st, 1865 by the Crystal Palace & South London Junction Railway as *Crystal Palace High Level* station and renamed as *Crystal Palace High Level & Upper Norwood* by the SE&CR on November 1st, 1898. The station was closed on January 1st, 1917, reopened on March 1st, 1919 and the name reverted back to *Crystal Palace High Level* by the SR on July 9th, 1923.

The destruction by fire of the Crystal Palace in 1936 led to a major decline in traffic and wartime damage caused the station to close between May 22nd, 1944 and March 4th, 1946. Requiring major engineering work that was considered as too expensive to be justified the station and the branch were closed by BR on September 20th, 1954. It was demolished in 1961 and the site redeveloped with housing.

Marcus Eavis/Online Transport Archive

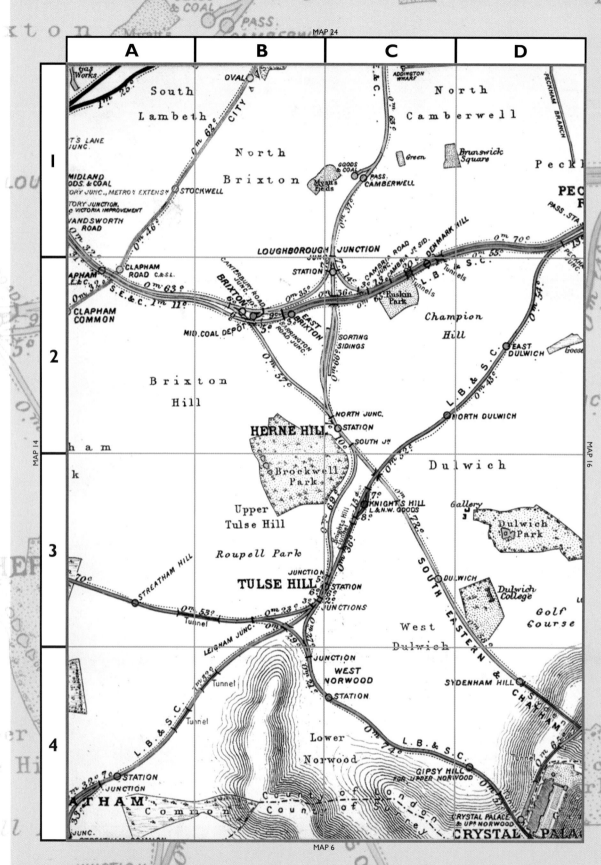

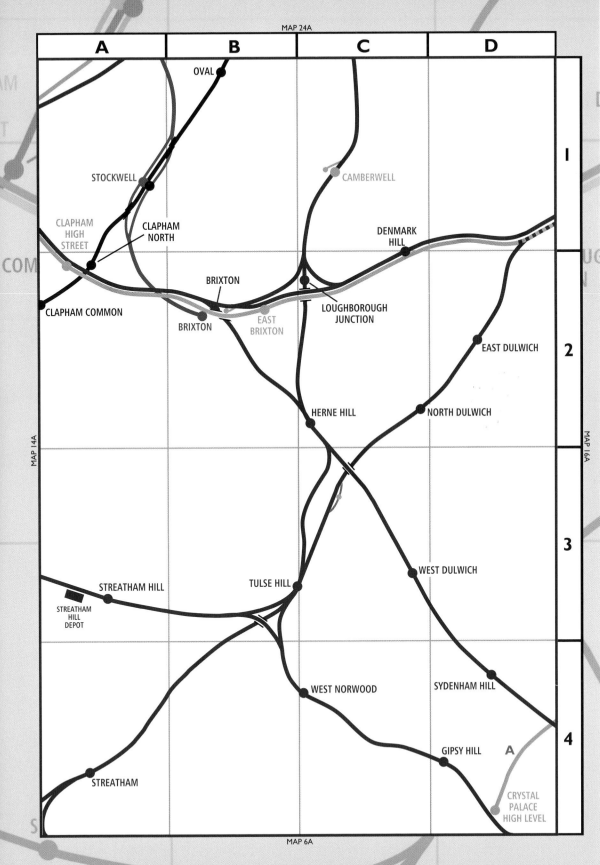

A | **B** | **C** | **D**

MAP 24A

OVAL

STOCKWELL

CAMBERWELL

CLAPHAM HIGH STREET

CLAPHAM NORTH

DENMARK HILL

CLAPHAM COMMON

BRIXTON

BRIXTON

EAST BRIXTON

LOUGHBOROUGH JUNCTION

EAST DULWICH

HERNE HILL

NORTH DULWICH

WEST DULWICH

STREATHAM HILL

STREATHAM HILL DEPOT

TULSE HILL

STREATHAM

WEST NORWOOD

SYDENHAM HILL

GIPSY HILL

A

CRYSTAL PALACE HIGH LEVEL

MAP 14A

MAP 16A

MAP 6A

Brixton station, looking east on June 25th, 2016. It was opened by the London, Chatham & Dover Railway on August 20th, 1862 as *Brixton*, renamed as *Brixton & South Stockwell* on May 1st, 1863 and reverted back to *Brixton* by the SR on July 9th, 1934.

Looking south at **Loughborough Junction station**, on July 23rd, 2016. The first part of the station, on the curve to *Brixton*, was opened by the LC&DR in October 1864 as *Loughborough Road* and following construction of the main line and Cambria spur to *Denmark Hill* the enlarged station was renamed as *Loughborough Junction* on December 1st, 1872.

Class 377 EMU No.**377449** and Class 319 EMU No.**319443** at **Tulse Hill station** on July 23rd, 2016. It was opened by the LB&SCR on October 1st, 1868.

LEGEND
CLOSED LINES
A CRYSTAL PALACE HIGH LEVEL BRANCH
Opened by the Crystal Palace and South London Junction Railway on August 1st, 1865, the line briefly closed during World War 1 between 1917 and 1919 and World War 2 between 1944 and 1946 before final closure by BR on September 20th, 1954.

MAP 16
1921

Looking north towards the tunnel at **Upper Sydenham station** on August 14th, 1954, just before the line closed. *(see Note under "Crystal Palace High Level" on Map 15)*

The station was opened on August 1st, 1884 by the London, Chatham & Dover Railway and, in similar fashion to *Crystal Palace High Level* on Map 15, was closed on January 1st, 1917, reopened on March 1st, 1919, closed by the SR on May 22nd, 1944, reopened on March 4th, 1946 and finally closed by BR on September 20th, 1954.

Gerald Druce/Online Transport Archive

Peckham Rye station, viewed here on March 15th, 1952, was opened by the LC&DR on December 1st, 1865 with the LB&SCR platforms opening on August 13th, 1866 *Gerald Druce/Online Transport Archive*

BR Class 415/1 4-EPB EMU No.5266 at **Bellingham Carriage Sidings** in 1988. *Phil Mackie*

A Pre-World War 2 view of **New Cross Gate MPD**. It was originally opened by the London & Croydon Railway on June 1st, 1839 and enlarged by the LB&SCR. The SR closed it as a running shed in June 1947 and it continued in use as an Engine Repair Depot until final closure by BR on May 23rd, 1949.

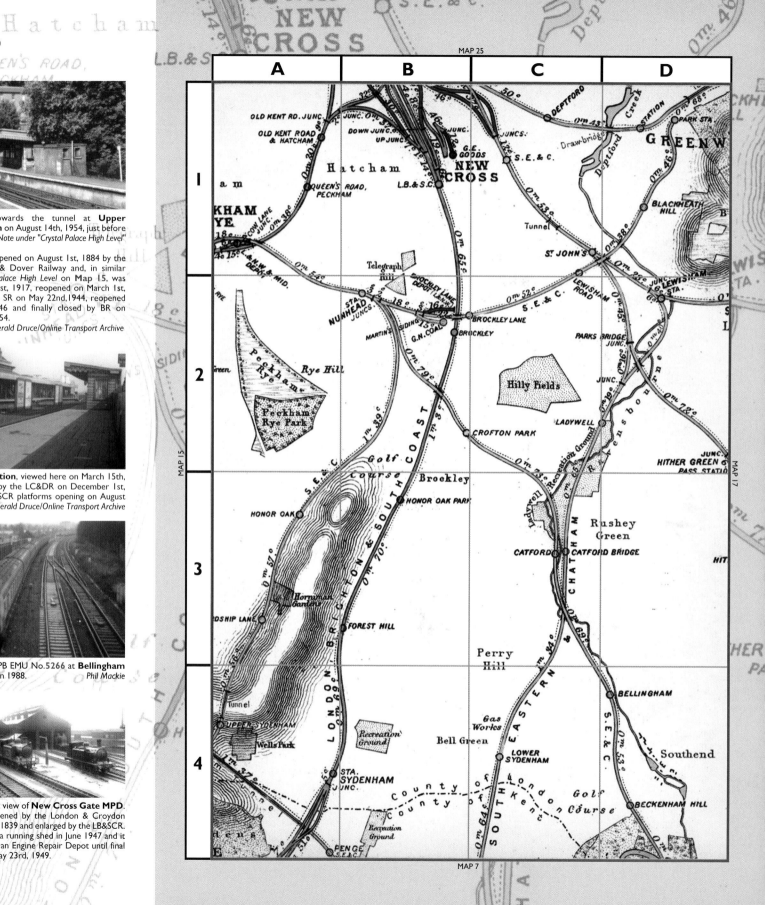

MAP 25A

A	B	C	D

DEPTFORD

GREENWICH

OLD KENT ROAD & HATCHAM

GREENWICH PARK

QUEENS ROAD PECKHAM

NEW CROSS

NEW CROSS GATE

DEPTFORD BRIDGE

1

PECKHAM RYE

A

BLACKHEATH HILL

ST JOHNS

ELVERSON ROAD

LEWISHAM ROAD

NUNHEAD

LEWISHAM

BROCKLEY LANE

BROCKLEY

2

LADYWELL

CROFTON PARK

B

HONOR OAK PARK

HONOR OAK

LORDSHIP LANE

CATFORD   CATFORD BRIDGE

3

FOREST HILL

UPPER SYDENHAM

BELLINGHAM

SYDENHAM

LOWER SYDENHAM

4

BECKENHAM HILL

PENGE EAST

MAP 15A

MAP 17A

MAP 7A

CATFORD   CATFORD BRIDGE

Class 465 EMU No.465913 at **Greenwich station**, on May 25th, 2016. The station was opened by the London & Greenwich Railway on April 12th, 1840 and replaced an earlier one opened on December 24th, 1838.

B2007 Stock Train No.149 arriving at **Lewisham DLR station** on May 14th, 2016. The station opened, along with the branch from *Island Gardens*, on December 3rd, 1999.

Looking south at **Catford Bridge station** on June 25th, 2016. Worked from the outset by the SER, it was opened by the Mid-Kent & North Kent Junction Railway on January 1st, 1857.

LEGEND
CLOSED LINES

A GREENWICH PARK BRANCH
Originally completed by the LC&DR as a branch from Nunhead in 1888 the line, and its four stations, was closed on January 1st, 1917. The line beyond Lewisham Road was abandoned by the SR on January 1st, 1926 but the section between Nunhead and Lewisham Road was reinstated on July 7th, 1929 and a new chord installed at the eastern end linking it to Lewisham

B CRYSTAL PALACE HIGH LEVEL BRANCH
Opened by the Crystal Palace and South London Junction Railway on August 1st, 1865, the line briefly closed during World War 1 between 1917 and 1919 and World War 2 between 1944 and 1946 before final closure by BR on September 20th, 1954.

MAP 17
1921

Eltham Well Hall station, viewed on June 15th, 1974. It was opened by the Blackheath Railway on May 1st, 1895 as *Well Hall*, renamed as *Well Hall for North Eltham* by the SE&CR on October 1st, 1916 and as *Eltham Well Hall* by the SR on September 26th, 1927.
Alan Young

Eltham Park station on June 15th, 1974. It was opened by the SE&CR on July 1st, 1908 as *Shooter's Hill & Eltham Park* and renamed as *Eltham Park* by the SR on September 26th, 1927.
Alan Young
  Both of the above stations were closed by BR on March 17th, 1985 and replaced by *Eltham*.

Grove Park station on May 5th, 1979. It was opened by the SER on November 1st, 1871.
Alan Young

Looking north at **Hither Green station** on May 5th, 1979. It was opened by the SER on June 1st, 1895.
Alan Young

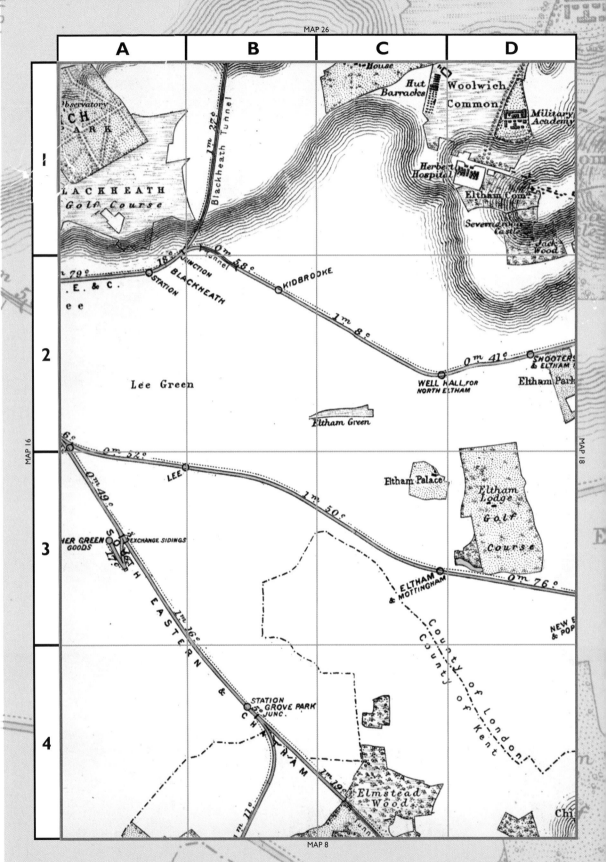

MAP 26A

A	B	C	D

1

BLACKHEATH

KIDBROOKE

ELTHAM PARK

2

ELTHAM

HITHER GREEN

HITHER GREEN DEPOT

LEE

3

MOTTINGHAM

GROVE PARK DEPOT

GROVE PARK

4

MAP 16A

MAP 18A

MAP 8A

GROVE PARK DEPOT

Eltham station, looking north, on May 14th, 2016. It was opened by BR on March 17th, 1985 and replaced two others which were both closed on the same day: *Eltham Well Hall* which was sited 220 yards to the west and *Eltham Park* 500 yards to the east.

Class 465 EMU No.**465024** entering **Mottingham station** on May 14th, 2016 on a service to Plumstead. The station was opened by the South Eastern Railway on September 1st, 1866 as *Eltham*, renamed as *Eltham & Mottingham* by the SE&CR on January 1st, 1892, as *Eltham for Mottingham* in April 1916, as *Eltham & Mottingham* in October 1922 and as *Mottingham* by the SR on September 26th, 1927.

Class 465 EMU No.**465245** at **Kidbrooke station** on May 21st, 2016. It was opened by the Blackheath Railway on May 1st, 1895.

Class 465 EMU No.**465165** at **Blackheath station** on May 14th, 2016. It was opened by the SER on July 30th, 1849.

MAP 18
1921

Falconwood station on February 23rd, 1979.
Alan Young

BR Class 415/2 EMU No.5355 at **Sidcup station** on March 3rd, 1979.
Alan Young

Welling station on February 23rd, 1979.
Alan Young

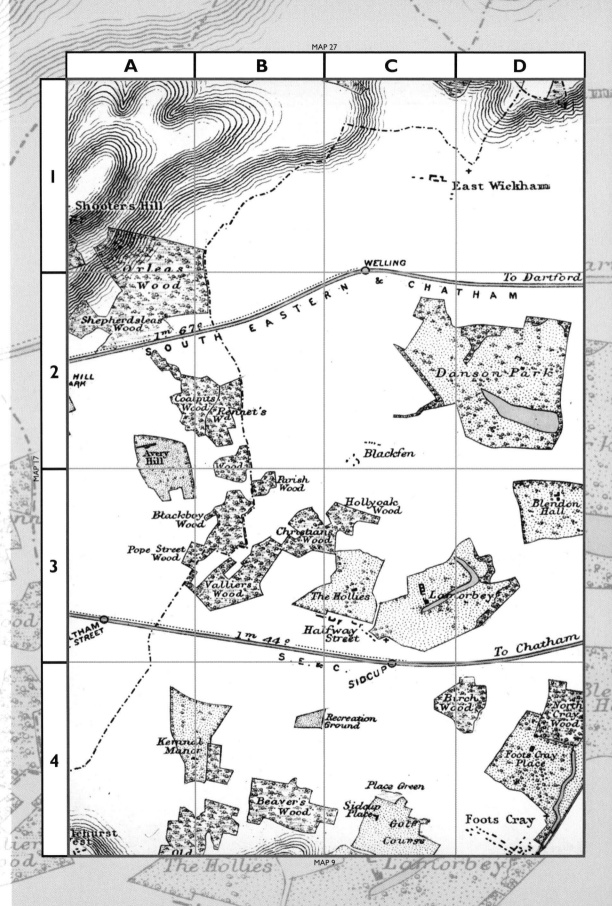

WELLING

MAP 27A

	A	B	C	D	

1

WELLING

FALCONWOOD

2

MAP 17A

3

NEW ELTHAM

ALBANY PARK

SIDCUP

4

MAP 9A

SIDCUP

Class 465 EMU No.465181 at **Falconwood station** on May 21st, 2016. The station was opened by the SR on January 1st, 1936.

Class 376 EMU No.376007 awaiting to depart from **Welling station** on May 21st, 2016. The station was opened by the Blackheath Railway on May 1st, 1895.

The 1988-constructed ticket office and entrance to **New Eltham station**, viewed on May 21st 2016. It was opened by the South Eastern Railway on April 1st, 1878 as *Pope Street*, renamed as *New Eltham & Pope Street* on January 1st, 1886 and as *New Eltham* by the SR on September 26th, 1927.

Class 465 EMU No.465011 at **Sidcup station** on May 21st, 2016. The station was opened by the SE&CR on September 1st, 1866 and was described as *Sidcup for Halfway Street* in some timetables.

MAP 19
1921

An interesting ticket dated November 2nd, 1959 and issued at **Hayes & Harlington station** for the conveyance of a perambulator at a cost of 14/9d.

This was just one type of a whole array of different tickets issued and an article* in the December 6th, 1956 edition of the *New Scientist* revealed that a sample investigation had found that, in view of the large range on offer, no less than 527,000,000 pre-printed tickets were held at BR's 5,600 selling points!

* *Tickets by Technology by RJ Eaton*

Looking west at **Hayes and Harlington station**, on May 30th, 1976. It was opened by the GWR on May 1st, 1864 as *Hayes* and renamed as *Hayes & Harlington* on November 22nd, 1897.　　　　*Alan Young*

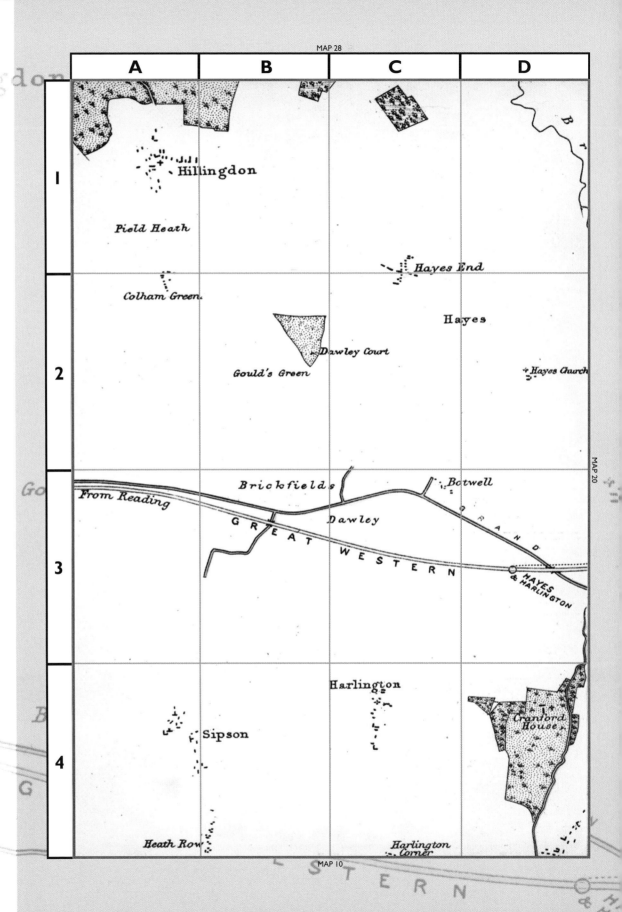

MAP 28

	A	B	C	D
1	Hillingdon · Field Heath			
2	Colham Green	Dawley Court · Gould's Green	Hayes End · Hayes · Hayes Church	
3	From Reading	Brickfields · Dawley · GREAT WESTERN	Botwell · GRAND	HAYES & HARLINGTON
4	Sipson · Heath Row		Harlington · Harlington Corner	Cranford House

MAP 10

A	B	C	D

1

2

3

4

GRAND UNION CANAL

HEATHROW JUNCTION*

A

HAH/NR BOUNDARY

HAYES & HARLINGTON

MAP 19A
January 1st, 2016

Looking west at **Hayes and Harlington station** on July 17th, 2016. It was opened by the GWR on May 1st, 1864 as *Hayes* and renamed as *Hayes & Harlington* on November 22nd, 1897.

STATIONS

HEATHROW JUNCTION was a temporary station opened when the tunnel leading to the airport collapsed during construction. It acted as a terminus for Heathrow Express trains from January 19th, 1998 until May 25th, 1998.

LEGEND

A The line and stations beyond the Boundary Point are the property of Heathrow Airport Holdings.

The Heathrow Express stations at *Heathrow Terminals 1, 2 & 3* and *Heathrow Terminal 4* both opened on May 25th, 1998 when the temporary station at *Heathrow Junction* – opened on January 19th, 1998 – closed for the second time (the service was suspended between January 31st and February 3rd, 1998 due to wheel damage).

Heathrow Terminals 1, 2 & 3 station was renamed as *Heathrow Central* and subsequently *Heathrow Terminals 2 & 3*

The joint Heathrow Express/LUL station at *Heathrow Terminal 5* opened on March 27th, 2008.

MAP 20
1921

Southall MPD viewed on September 25th, 1963. The first shed on this site was originally opened by the GWR in 1884 but was demolished in 1953 and replaced with the building in the illustration. The shed closed to steam on January 3rd, 1966 and continued in use as a DMU depot for another ten years.

It was not demolished and is now known as the *Southall Railway Centre*, a base for three separate railway-orientated concerns.　*WT Stubbs*

A ticket for travel between *Langley (Bucks)* and **Southall station** issued on July 1st, 1970.

517 Class 0-4-2T No.833 auto-coach at **Trumpers Crossing Halt for South Hanwell & Osterley Park** in c1906/7. It was opened by the GWR on July 1st, 1904, closed on March 22nd, 1915, reopened on April 12th, 1920 and finally closed on February 1st, 1926.　*John Alsop*

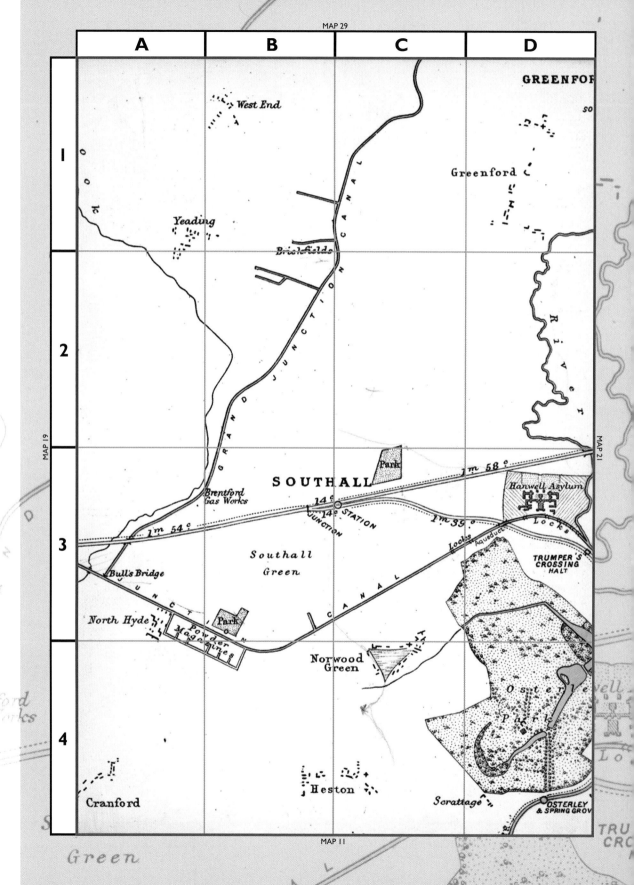

1

2

RIVER
BRENT

3

SOUTHALL

A

TRUMPER'S CROSSING HALT

4

GRAND UNION
CANAL

OSTERLEY

MAP 20A
January 1st, 2016

Southall station, looking west, on July 17th, 2016. It was opened by the GWR on May 1st, 1839.

One of the unusual bi-lingual English/Gurmukhī signs at **Southall station**, viewed on July 17th, 2016. They had been installed in the late 1990s but, following complaints from other ethnic groups, in 2007 the train train operator decided to remove them!

Osterley tube station on July 17th, 2016. It was opened by the LPTB on March 25th, 1934 and replaced *Osterley & Spring Grove* which was sited about 320 yards to the east and opened by the District Railway on May 1st, 1883.

LEGEND

A BRENTFORD BRANCH
Opened by the GWR on July 18th, 1859 and closed to passengers on May 4th, 1942, the line has been lifted beyond Brentford Goods and is currently used to serve an aggregate depot and refuse transfer station.

s.

MAP 21
1921

The Grade II listed station building at **North Ealing** on June 3rd, 1956. It was opened by the District Railway on June 23rd, 1903. *Marcus Eavis/Online Transport Archive*

A single-car unit on Platform 5 at **Acton Town tube station** on an unknown date. The station was opened by the District Railway on July 1st, 1879 as *Mill Hill Park*. and renamed as *Acton Town* on March 1st, 1910.

The Class G23 single-car unit was engaged on the shuttle service to *South Acton* which was withdrawn on February 28th, 1959. *J Joyce/Online Transport Archive*

Ealing Common (District Line) Depot viewed on November 18th, 1990. The 11-road shed was opened in 1905. *Philip Stuart*

Ex-GWR Class 0-6-0PT No.**5418** at **Ealing Broadway** on an unknown date.
Marcus Eavis/Online Transport Archive

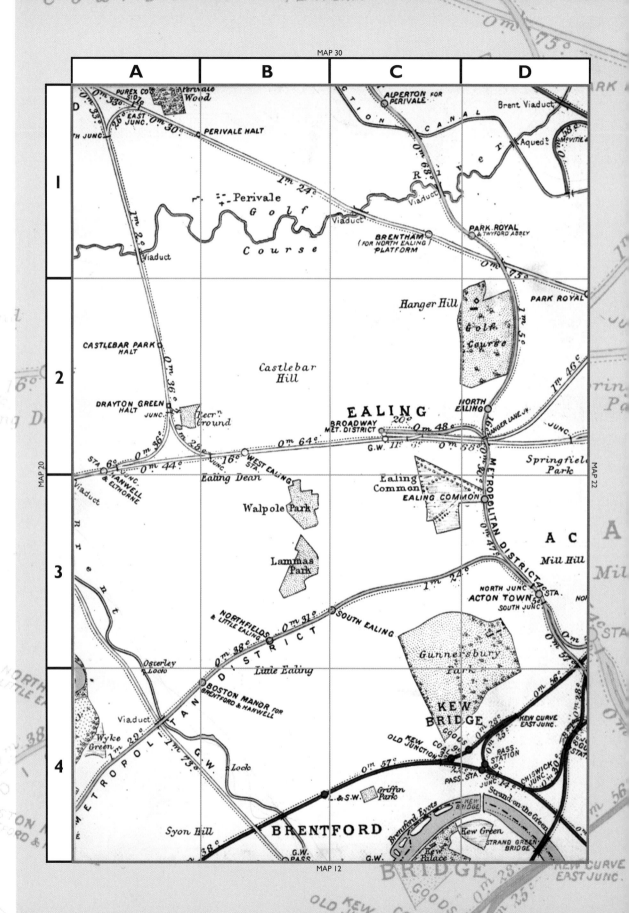

MAP

	A	**B**	**C**	**D**

ALPERTON

PERIVALE HALT

PERIVALE

SOUTH GREENFORD

RIVER BRENT

PARK ROYAL & TWYFORD ABBEY

BENTHAM FOR NORTH EALING & GREYSTOKE PARK

HANGER LANE

PARK ROYAL WEST HALT

PARK ROYAL

PARK ROYAL (GWR)

CASTLE BAR PARK

DRAYTON GREEN

WEST EALING

EALING BROADWAY

NORTH EALING

WEST ACTON

HANWELL

MAP 20A

EALING COMMON

EALING COMMON DEPOT

ACTON TOWN

SOUTH EALING

NORTHFIELDS

NORTHFIELDS DEPOT

BOSTON MANOR

RIVER BRENT

MAP 22A

GUNNERSBURY

KEW BRIDGE

BRENTFORD

A

RIVER THAMES

KEW BRIDGE

BRENTFORD (GWR)

SOUTH EALING

Looking east at **Boston Manor tube station** on February 22nd, 2014. It was opened by the District Railway on May 1st, 1883 as *Boston Road* and renamed as *Boston Manor* on December 11th, 1911. The station was extensively rebuilt in the *art deco* style in the mid-1930s and granted Grade II listed status in 2002.

In 2013 the station also featured on a postage stamp celebrating the 150th Anniversary of the first London underground train journey.

Gunnersbury station, looking north, on May 21st, 2016. It was opened by the L&SWR on January 1st, 1869 as *Brentford Road* and renamed as *Gunnersbury* on November 1st, 1871.

The District Line platforms at **Ealing Broadway tube station** viewed on February 22nd, 2014. The "through" station was opened by the GWR on December 1st, 1838 and on July 1st, 1879 the District Railway extended its branch from *Turnham Green* and constructed its own station consisting of bay platforms on the north side. In 1920 the Central Line was accommodated with two more bay platforms built between the two stations and in BR days they were all amalgamated into one station.

LEGEND

A BRENTFORD BRANCH

Opened by the GWR on July 18th, 1859 and closed to passengers on May 4th, 1942, the line has been lifted beyond Brentford Goods and is currently used to serve an aggregate depot and refuse transfer station.

MAP 22
1921

MAP 31

A Central Line train at **White City tube station** on March 30th, 1957. *Marcus Eavis/Online Transport*

BR Class 2 2-6-0 No.78063 in the yard at **Willesden MPD** on February 21st, 1965. The shed was opened by the L&NWR in 1873 and closed by BR on August 27th, 1965, the site being later utilized for a Freightliner terminal. *KCH Fairey*

A general view of the large shed complex at **Old Oak Common MPD** on July 3rd, 1963. It was opened by the GWR on March 17th, 1906 and BR closed it to steam on March 22nd, 1965. A diesel depot was subsequently established and the site has been in continuous use for servicing DMUs and EMUs since then. *WT Stubbs*

A tube train entering the 14-road carriage shed at **White City (Central Line) Depot** on January 26th, 1991. *Philip Stuart*

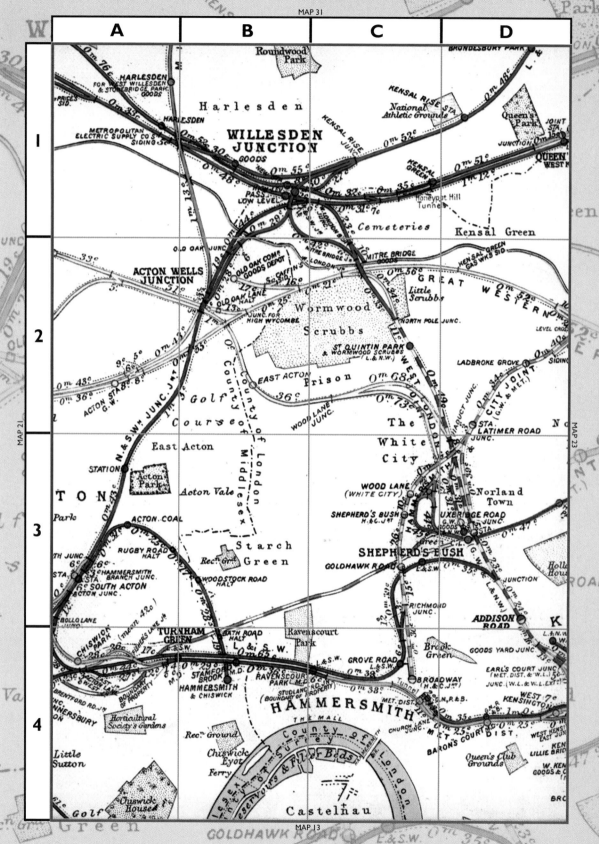

MAP 22A
January 1st, 2016

A	**B**	**C**	**D**	

BRONDESBURY PARK

KENSAL RISE

QUEEN'S PARK **1**

HARLESDEN

WILLESDEN JUNCTION DEPOT

WILLESDEN JUNCTION

KENSAL GREEN

HST & HEATHROW EXPRESS DEPOT

NORTH POLE DEPOT

NORTH ACTON

OLD OAK LANE HALT

ST QUINTIN PARK & WORMWOOD SCRUBBS

LADBROKE GROVE **2**

ACTON MAIN LINE

EAST ACTON

LATIMER ROAD

ACTON CENTRAL

WHITE CITY

WOOD LANE (LUL)

WOOD LANE (CLR)

WHITE CITY (MET/GWR)

HOLLAND PARK

SHEPHERD'S BUSH MARKET

SHEPHERD'S BUSH (WLR)

SHEPHERD'S BUSH (LOL) **3**

RUGBY ROAD HALT

A

UXBRIDGE ROAD

SHEPHERD'S BUSH (CLR)

SOUTH ACTON

WOODSTOCK ROAD HALT

GOLDHAWK ROAD

SHEPHERD'S BUSH (LSWR)

B

KENSINGTON (OLYMPIA)

CHISWICK PARK

BATH ROAD HALT

STAMFORD BROOK

GROVE ROAD

HAMMERSMITH DEPOT

TURNHAM GREEN

HAMMERSMITH & CHISWICK

RAVENSCOURT PARK

HAMMERSMITH (MET/GWR)

WEST KENSINGTON

HAMMERSMITH

RIVER THAMES

BARONS COURT **4**

Car No.21350 leading on an S7 Stock Hammersmith and City Line train at **Shepherd's Bush Market tube station** on July 26th, 2014. The station was opened by the Hammersmith & City Railway on April 1st, 1914 as *Shepherd's Bush* and renamed as *Shepherd's Bush Market* on October 12th, 2008.

Car No.21355 leading on an S7 Stock clockwise Circle Line train at **Wood Lane tube station** on July 26th, 2014. It was opened on October 12th, 2008.

Looking west at **Kensal Green station** on June 4th, 2016. It was opened by the L&NWR on October 1st, 1916.

LEGEND
CLOSED LINES

A HAMMERSMITH & CHISWICK BRANCH
Opened by the North & South West Junction Railway on May 1st, 1857 and closed to passengers by the L&SWR on January 1st, 1917, the line was totally closed by BR on May 3rd, 1965.

B GROVE PARK – SHEPHERDS BUSH
Opened by the L&SWR on January 1st, 1869 and closed on June 3rd, 1916, the line was finally abandoned by the SR in 1930.

MAP 23
1921

An Earls Court-bound train waiting alongside **Kensington South** Main signalbox on March 17th, 1956.
Marcus Eavis/Online Transport Archive

Ex-Metropolitan Railway Bo-Bo Electric Locomotive No.13 *Dick Whittington* at **Baker Street tube station** on a service to Aylesbury on an unknown date. The locomotives were introduced in 1925, utilizing some parts from a previously-constructed class, and eventually numbered some twenty. Of these fifteen survived to 1953 and were overhauled and utilized until the electrification to Amersham was completed in 1961. No.13 was scrapped in the following year.
J Joyce/Online Transport Archive

South Kensington tube station opened in three parts. The sub-surface platforms were opened by the Metropolitan Railway on December 24th, 1868, joined by the District Railway on July 10th, 1871, and the deep-tube Great Northern, Piccadilly & Brompton Railway arrived on January 8th, 1907.

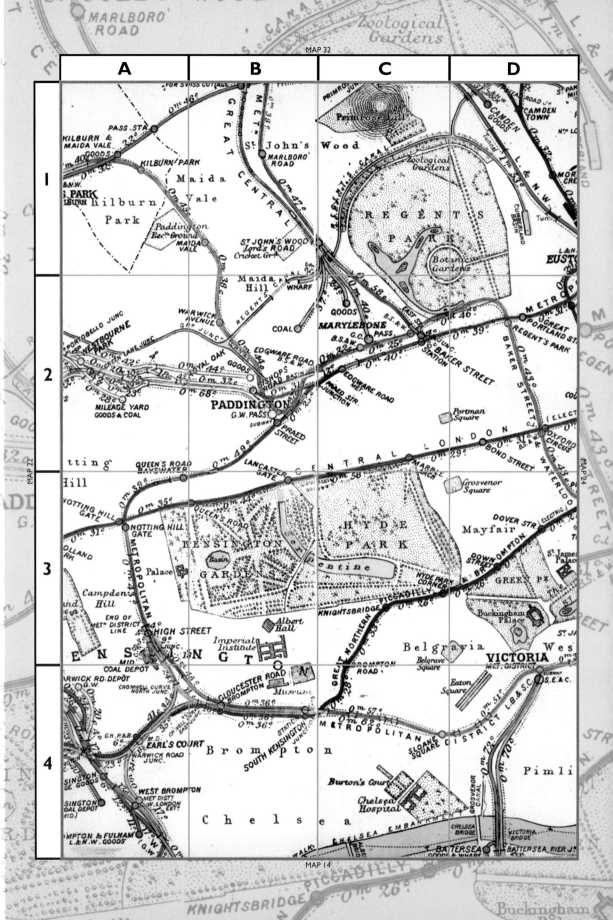

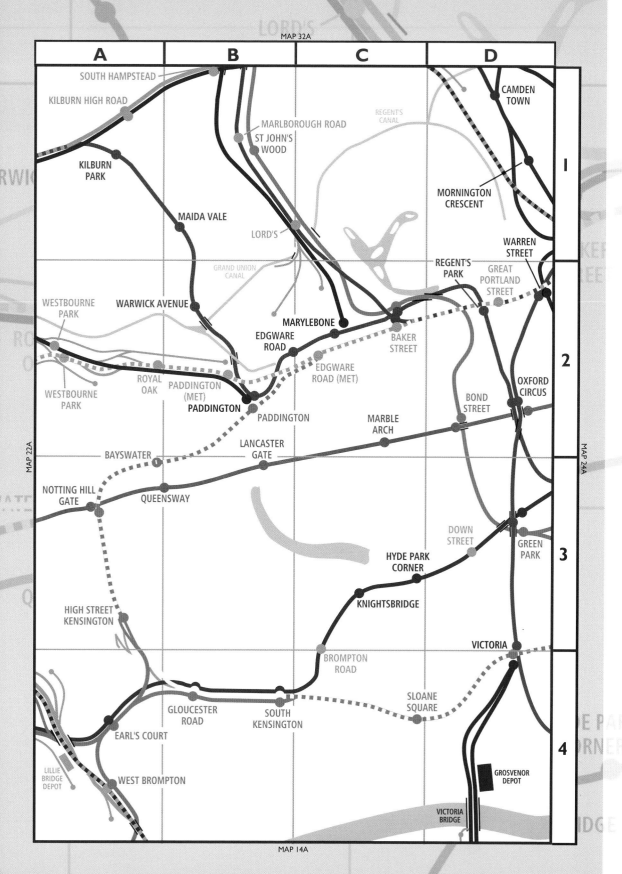

MAP 32A

	A	B	C	D	

SOUTH HAMPSTEAD
KILBURN HIGH ROAD

CAMDEN TOWN

REGENT'S CANAL

MARLBOROUGH ROAD
ST JOHN'S WOOD

1

KILBURN PARK

MORNINGTON CRESCENT

MAIDA VALE

LORD'S

WARREN STREET

REGENT'S PARK

GREAT PORTLAND STREET

WESTBOURNE PARK

WARWICK AVENUE

GRAND UNION CANAL

MARYLEBONE

EDGWARE ROAD

BAKER STREET

2

MAP 22A

ROYAL OAK

WESTBOURNE PARK

PADDINGTON (MET)

PADDINGTON

EDGWARE ROAD (MET)

BOND STREET

OXFORD CIRCUS

MAP 24A

PADDINGTON

MARBLE ARCH

BAYSWATER

LANCASTER GATE

NOTTING HILL GATE

QUEENSWAY

DOWN STREET

GREEN PARK

3

HYDE PARK CORNER

KNIGHTSBRIDGE

HIGH STREET KENSINGTON

VICTORIA

BROMPTON ROAD

SLOANE SQUARE

GLOUCESTER ROAD

SOUTH KENSINGTON

EARL'S COURT

4

LILLIE BRIDGE DEPOT

WEST BROMPTON

GROSVENOR DEPOT

VICTORIA BRIDGE

MAP 14A

The main train shed at **London Marylebone station** viewed on June 4th, 2016. It was opened by the Great Central Railway on March 15th, 1899 and was the last main line station to be built in London. During the 1980s it was threatened with total closure and conversion to a coach station but, following many objections, this plan was abandoned and it was subsequently refurbished.

Looking north at **High Street Kensington tube station** on July 30th, 2016. It was opened by the Metropolitan Railway on July 3rd, 1871 as *Kensington High Street* and renamed as *High Street, Kensington* by the Metropolitan District Railway prior to 1904.

Looking north at **West Brompton station** on July 30th, 2016. It was opened by the West London Extension Joint Railway on September 1st, 1866, closed on October 21st, 1940 and reopened on June 1st, 1999.

Class 378 EMU No.**378204** at **South Hampstead station** on August 6th, 2016. It was opened by the L&NWR on June 2nd, 1879 as *Loudoun Road*, closed on January 1st, 1917 and reopened on July 10th, 1922 as *South Hampstead*.

MAP 24
1921

Ex-LNER Class J50 0-6-0T No.68961 approaching **Farringdon station** from the north on an unknown date. The station was originally known as *Farringdon Street* and then *Farringdon & High Holborn* until 1936.
Marcus Eavis/Online Transport Archive

Postcard showing a pre-grouping view of **Liverpool Street station**.
Cty Keith Turner

BRITISH RAILWAYS

LONDON SUBURBAN PASSENGER SERVICES

FROM AND TO
LIVERPOOL STREET

12th SEPTEMBER 1960
to 11th JUNE 1961
or until further notice

NORTH EAST LONDON ELECTRIFICATION
The services between LIVERPOOL STREET and CHINGFORD, ENFIELD TOWN, HERTFORD (EAST), BUNTINGFORD and BISHOP'S STORTFORD, PALACE GATES and NORTH WOOLWICH will be revised on 21st November — for details see later announcements

FOURPENCE

A pocket timetable issued on November 12th, 1960, embracing the changeover from steam to electric traction on **Liverpool Street** suburban services which took place on November 21st, 1960.

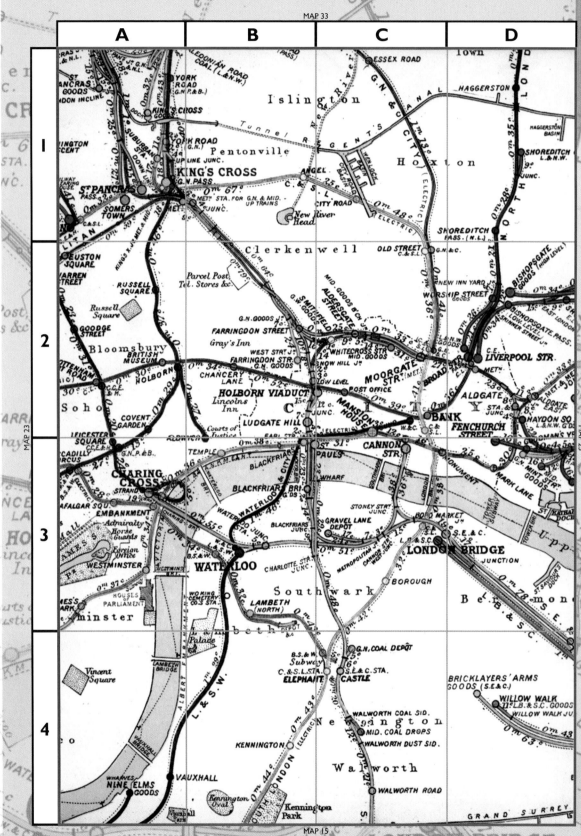

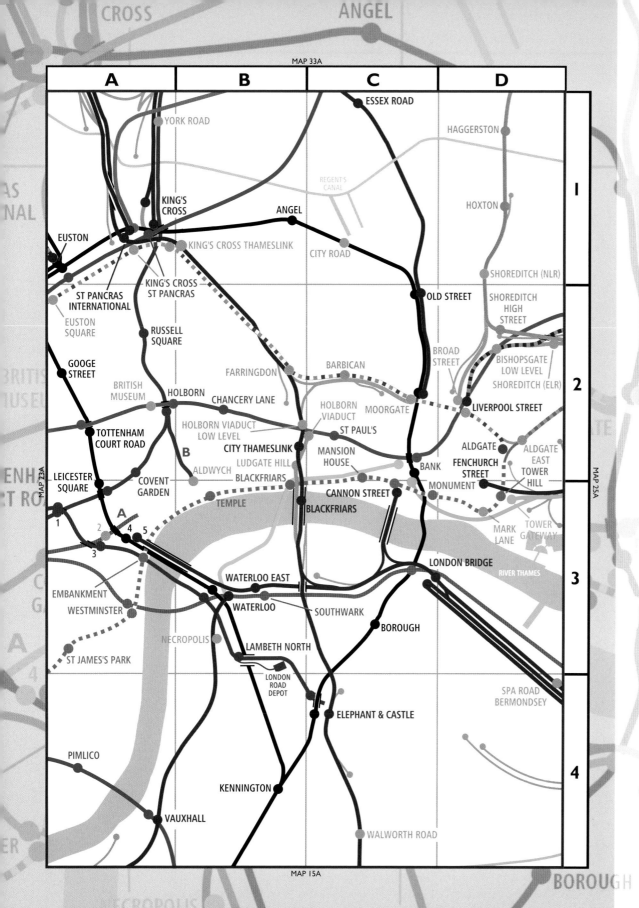

YORK ROAD

ESSEX ROAD

HAGGERSTON

REGENT'S CANAL

KING'S CROSS

ANGEL

HOXTON

EUSTON

KING'S CROSS THAMESLINK

ST PANCRAS INTERNATIONAL

KING'S CROSS ST PANCRAS

CITY ROAD

SHOREDITCH (NLR)

EUSTON SQUARE

RUSSELL SQUARE

OLD STREET

SHOREDITCH HIGH STREET

GOOGE STREET

BRITISH MUSEUM

FARRINGDON

BARBICAN

BROAD STREET

BISHOPSGATE LOW LEVEL

SHOREDITCH (ELR)

HOLBORN

CHANCERY LANE

HOLBORN VIADUCT

MOORGATE

LIVERPOOL STREET

TOTTENHAM COURT ROAD

HOLBORN VIADUCT LOW LEVEL

ST PAUL'S

B

CITY THAMESLINK

MANSION HOUSE

LEICESTER SQUARE

LUDGATE HILL

ALDWYCH

BLACKFRIARS

BANK

ALDGATE

FENCHURCH STREET

ALDGATE EAST

TOWER HILL

COVENT GARDEN

MONUMENT

A

TEMPLE

CANNON STREET

BLACKFRIARS

MARK LANE

TOWER GATEWAY

1 2 4 5

3

EMBANKMENT

WATERLOO EAST

LONDON BRIDGE

RIVER THAMES

WESTMINSTER

WATERLOO

SOUTHWARK

ST JAMES'S PARK

NECROPOLIS

BOROUGH

LAMBETH NORTH

LONDON ROAD DEPOT

SPA ROAD BERMONDSEY

ELEPHANT & CASTLE

PIMLICO

KENNINGTON

VAUXHALL

WALWORTH ROAD

Class 395 "Javelin" EMU No.**395006** awaiting departure from **St Pancras International station** on August 30th, 2011. The station was opened by the Midland Railway on October 1st, 1868 and was extensively rebuilt between 2001 and 2007 to accommodate HS1.

Class 466 EMU No.**466012** on Platform 6 at **London Bridge station** on April 20th, 2011. This station is in the process of being completely rebuilt. The project started in 2013 and is due to be finished in 2018.

Class 379 EMU No.**379005** and Class 317 EMU No.**317501** at the buffer stops at **Liverpool Street station** on April 20th, 2011.

STATIONS
1. PICCADILLY CIRCUS [BAKERLOO AND PICCADILLY LINES]
2. CHARING CROSS [JUBILEE LINE] Opened on March 1st, 1979 and closed on November 20th, 1999. (See note **A** in Legend)
3. CHARING CROSS [BAKERLOO LINE]
4. CHARING CROSS [NORTHERN LINE]
5. CHARING CROSS [NATIONAL RAIL]

LEGEND

A The Jubilee line terminated at Charing Cross from March 1st, 1979 until the extension from Green Park to Stratford opened on November 20th, 1999. Charing Cross station closed on that day and the remaining short stub is occasionally used for reversing trains and stabling stock.
B The Aldwych branch and station closed on September 30th, 1994 and is currently used as a location for filming tube station scenes.

MAP 25
1921

The entrance to **Bow Road tube station** on an unrecorded date. *Bow Road* underground station was opened in 1902 by the Whitechapel & Bow Railway and the booking hall is now a Grade II listed building.
Marcus Eavis/Online Transport Archive

Millwall Junction shed, viewed on March 26th, 1937. It had been constructed as a goods shed by the GNR and was purchased by the GER in 1871 for conversion to an engine and carriage shed. The building was closed as a running shed by the LNER in May 1926 and had been reverted back to goods use at the time of this photograph.
WA Camwell

Looking north at **Cambridge Heath station** on July 25th, 1975. It was opened by the GER on May 27th, 1872, closed on May 22nd, 1916, and reopened on May 5th, 1919. It was closed between July 27th, 1984 and September 1984, due to a fire and for rebuilding between February 17th, 1986 and March 16th, 1986.
Alan Young

Bethnal Green station viewed on September 28th, 1974. It was opened by the GER on May 24th, 1872 as *Bethnal Green Junction* and renamed as *Bethnal Green* by the L&NER in December 1946.
Alan Young

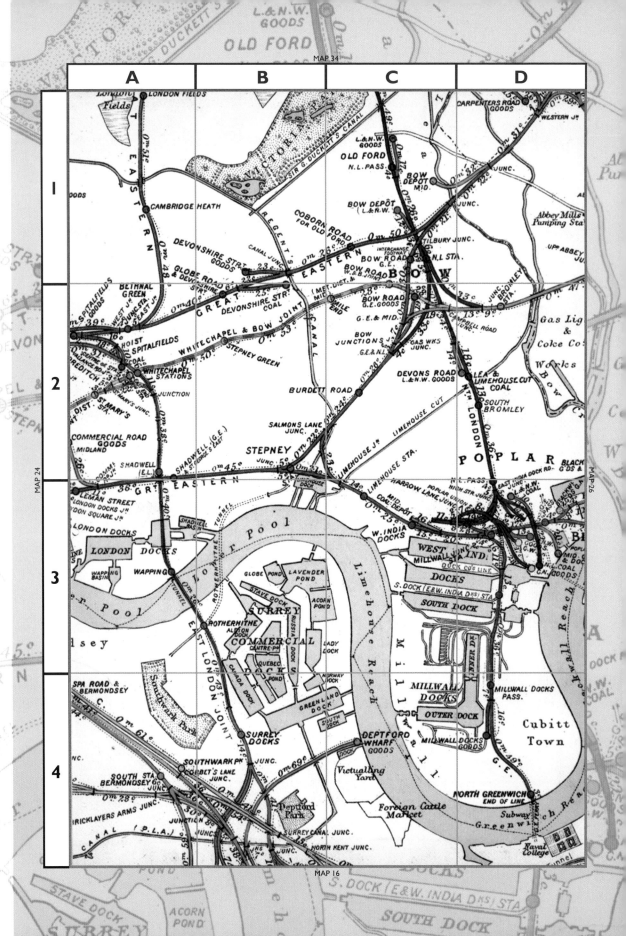

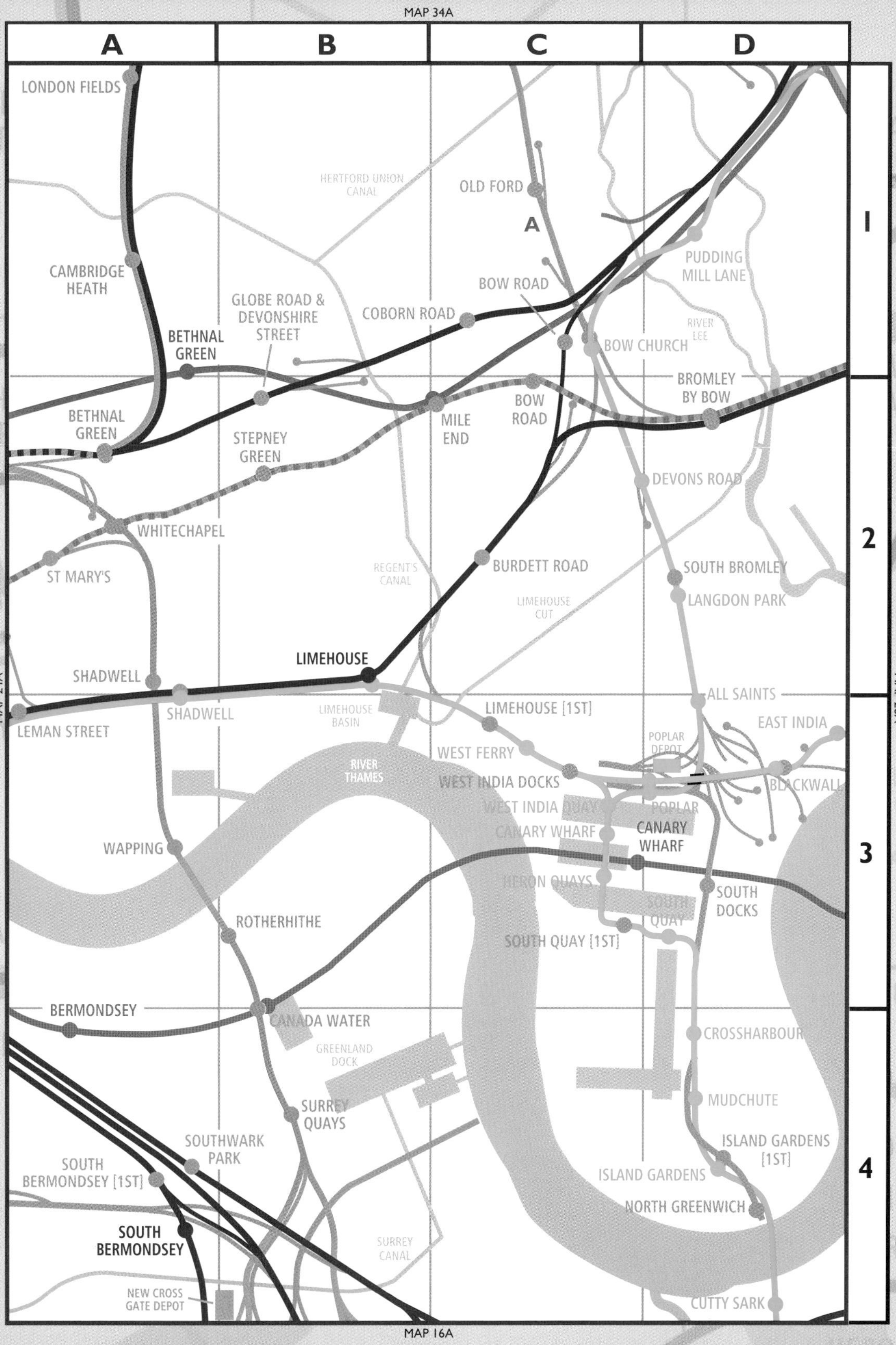

MAP 34A

A	B	C	D

MAP 24A

MAP 26A

1

LONDON FIELDS

CAMBRIDGE HEATH

HERTFORD UNION CANAL

OLD FORD

A

BETHNAL GREEN

GLOBE ROAD & DEVONSHIRE STREET

COBORN ROAD

BOW ROAD

PUDDING MILL LANE

RIVER LEE

BOW CHURCH

BETHNAL GREEN

STEPNEY GREEN

MILE END

BOW ROAD

BROMLEY BY BOW

2

WHITECHAPEL

ST MARY'S

REGENT'S CANAL

BURDETT ROAD

LIMEHOUSE CUT

DEVONS ROAD

SOUTH BROMLEY

LANGDON PARK

SHADWELL

LIMEHOUSE

3

SHADWELL

LIMEHOUSE BASIN

LIMEHOUSE [1ST]

WEST FERRY

ALL SAINTS

EAST INDIA

LEMAN STREET

RIVER THAMES

WEST INDIA DOCKS

POPLAR DEPOT

WEST INDIA QUAY

POPLAR

BLACKWALL

WAPPING

CANARY WHARF

CANARY WHARF

HERON QUAYS

SOUTH QUAY

SOUTH DOCKS

ROTHERHITHE

SOUTH QUAY [1ST]

BERMONDSEY

CANADA WATER

GREENLAND DOCK

CROSSHARBOUR

4

SOUTHWARK PARK

SURREY QUAYS

MUDCHUTE

SOUTH BERMONDSEY [1ST]

ISLAND GARDENS [1ST]

ISLAND GARDENS

SOUTH BERMONDSEY

SURREY CANAL

NORTH GREENWICH

NEW CROSS GATE DEPOT

CUTTY SARK

MAP 16A

The entrance to **Rotherhithe station** viewed on April 2nd, 2016. It was opened by the East London Railway on December 7th, 1869 and temporarily closed between 1995 and 1998, and December 22nd, 2007 and April 27th, 2010 for engineering works.

Looking north at **Surrey Quays station** on July 9th, 2016. It was opened by the East London Railway on December 7th, 1869 as *Deptford Road*, renamed as *Surrey Docks* on July 17th, 1911 and as *Surrey Quays* on October 24th, 1985.

B92AV Stock Train No.**36** at **Poplar DLR station** on July 16th, 2016. The station opened on August 31st, 1987.

LEGEND
CLOSED LINES
A VICTORIA PARK – BOW
Opened by the North London Railway on September 26th, 1850 and closed to passengers during World War 2 on May 15th, 1944, the line was totally closed by BR on October 3rd, 1983

MAP 35

MAP 26
1921

North Woolwich station viewed during 1975. It was opened by the Eastern Counties & Thames Junction Railway on June 14th, 1847 and was closed from May 29th, 1994 until October 29th, 1995 for engineering work on the Jubilee extension before final closure on December 9th, 2006.

Between 1984 and November 2008 the former station building and one platform were in use as the "North Woolwich Old Station Museum". *Phil Mackie*

A ticket issued by the Port of London Authority. The Authority was established in 1906 and became responsible for the extensive railway system which was mainly sidings and goods facilities but also embraced passenger services too. **Custom House station** was on the LNER line from Canning Town and was opened on December 1st, 1855 by the Eastern Counties Railway and closed by Railtrack on May 29th, 1994.

It was reopened on October 29th, 1995 and finally closed on December 9th, 2006.

Manor Way station was sited within the docks complex and was opened by the London and St Katherine's Dock Company in November 1880 and closed in 1940. The Port of London Authority railway system closed on May 1st, 1970.

The entrance to **Stratford Market station** viewed in the 1950s. The station was opened on June 14th, 1847 by the Eastern Counties Railway as *Stratford Bridge* and renamed as *Stratford Market* by the GER on November 1st, 1880. The station was closed by BR on May 6th, 1957 and the trackbed subsequently used for the DLR. *Stratford High Street DLR station* was built on the site and opened on August 31st, 2011. The entrance building is still extant.

Marcus Eavis/Online Transport Archive

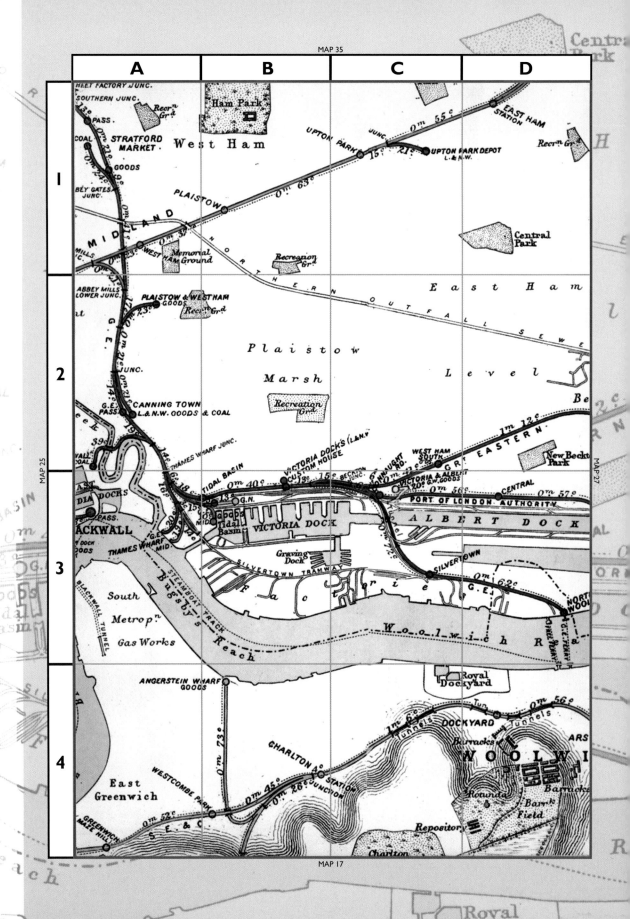

MAP 17

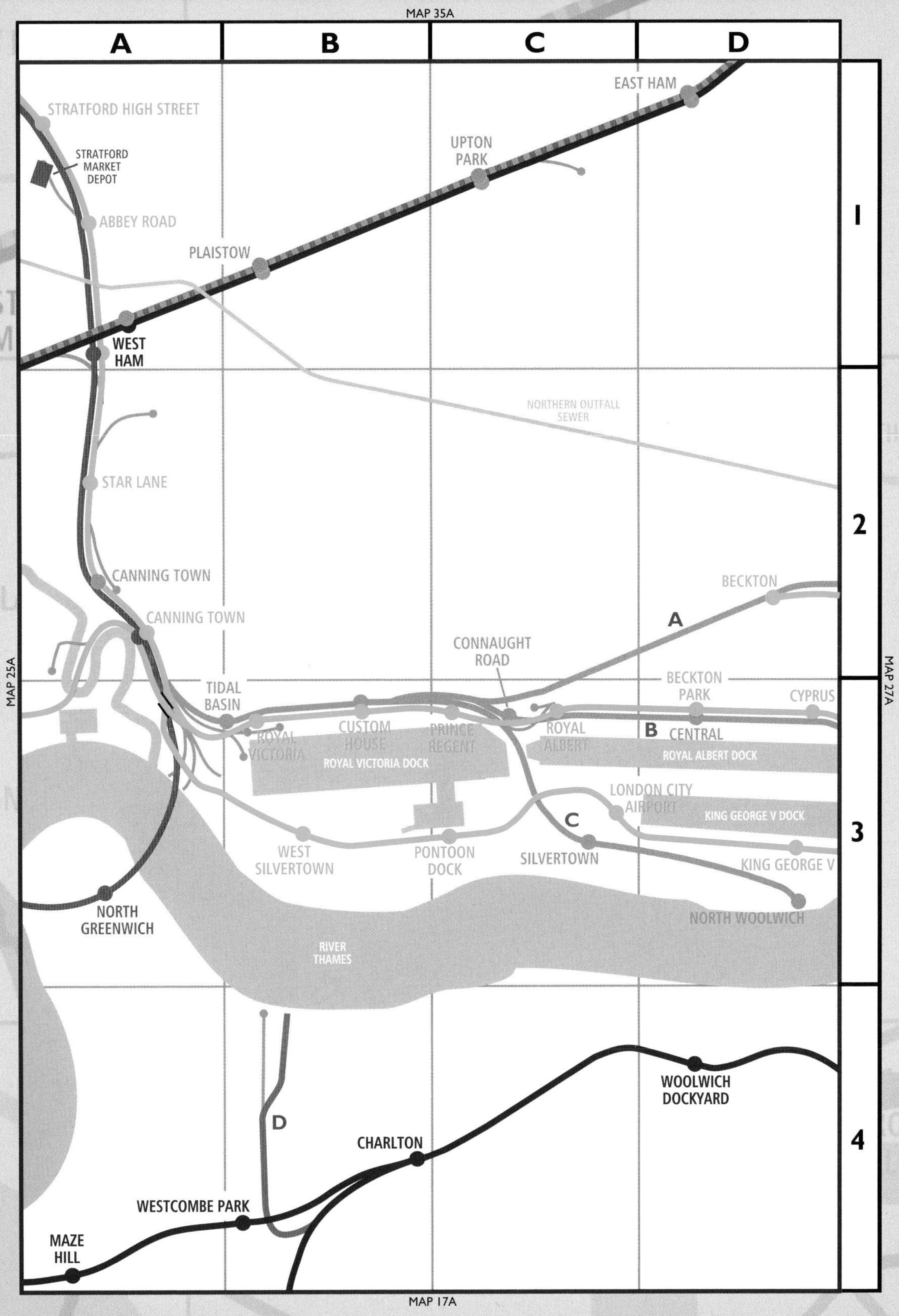

Map labels:

MAP 35A

| A | B | C | D |

STRATFORD HIGH STREET

STRATFORD MARKET DEPOT

ABBEY ROAD

PLAISTOW

WEST HAM

EAST HAM

UPTON PARK

STAR LANE

NORTHERN OUTFALL SEWER

CANNING TOWN

CANNING TOWN

BECKTON

CONNAUGHT ROAD

A

TIDAL BASIN

CUSTOM HOUSE

PRINCE REGENT

BECKTON PARK

CYPRUS

ROYAL VICTORIA

ROYAL ALBERT

B CENTRAL

ROYAL ALBERT DOCK

ROYAL VICTORIA DOCK

LONDON CITY AIRPORT

KING GEORGE V DOCK

WEST SILVERTOWN

PONTOON DOCK

SILVERTOWN

C

KING GEORGE V

NORTH GREENWICH

NORTH WOOLWICH

RIVER THAMES

WOOLWICH DOCKYARD

D

CHARLTON

WESTCOMBE PARK

MAZE HILL

MAP 25A

MAP 27A

MAP 17A

1 2 3 4

West Ham DLR station on May 14th, 2016 with B2007 Stock Train No.130 on a service to Stratford.

The station was originally opened by BR on May 14th, 1979 as part of the North London Line project but was closed between May 29th, 1994 and October 29th, 1995 for Jubilee Line work. The Jubilee Line platforms, on the left, opened on May 14th, 1999 and the North London Line platforms closed on December 10th, 2006 when the line was given over to the Docklands Light Railway. It opened as a DLR station on August 31st, 2011.

Class 465 EMU No.465195 at **Charlton station**, on May 21st, 2016. The station was opened by the South Eastern Railway on July 30th, 1849. It was renamed as *Charlton Junction* in 1877/8 and reverted to *Charlton* by the SR in 1928/9.

LEGEND
CLOSED LINES

A CUSTOM HOUSE - BECKTON BRANCH
Opened by the Gas Light & Coke Company on October 14th, 1872 to serve Beckton Gas Works the line closed to passengers on December 29th, 1940 and totally on February 22nd, 1971.

B CUSTOM HOUSE - GALLIONS BRANCH
Opened by the London & St Katherine Dock Company in 1880, closed to passengers on September 9th, 1940 and totally on April 17th, 1966.

C NORTH WOOLWICH BRANCH
Opened by the Eastern Counties & Thames Junction Railway on June 14th, 1847 and closed to passengers on December 10th, 2006 with part of the trackbed from east of Custom House station to North Woolwich retained for use as the route of Crossrail 1.

FREIGHT LINE

D ANGERSTEIN WHARF BRANCH
Built by John Angerstein and leased to the SER from October 30th, 1852 until 1898 when it was bought outright, it is currently used for transporting sea-dredged aggregates.

MAP 27
1921

The signal box and level crossing at **Abbey Wood station** on September 2nd, 1973. They were removed in the 1970s to make way for a flyover and the station entrance, visible on the left, was demolished and rebuilt in the 1980s. The station is currently being remodelled again, this time to accommodate Crossrail 1.
Phil Mackie

Another view of **Abbey Wood station**, looking west towards the level crossing on May 29th, 1974. It was opened by the SER on July 30th, 1849.   *Alan Young*

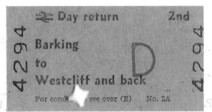

Barking station was opened by the London, Tilbury & Southend Railway on April 13th, 1854. This ticket was issued on May 13th, 1986.

Dagenham Dock station viewed on September 23rd, 1973. It was opened by the London, Tilbury & Southend Railway on July 1st, 1908.   *Alan Young*

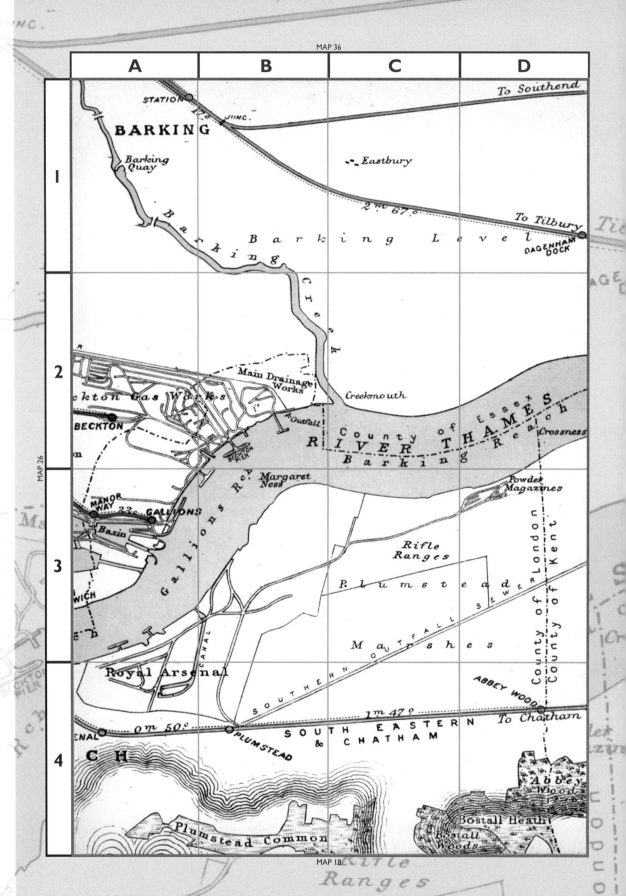

A	B	C	D

BARKING

UPNEY

BECONTREE

1

DAGENHAM DOCK

2

A
BECKTON

BECKTON DEPOT

GALLIONS REACH

MANOR WAY B GALLIONS

3

ABBEY WOOD

PLUMSTEAD

WOOLWICH ARSENAL

4

MAP 27A
January 1st, 2016

Looking west along the platform at **Upney tube station** on April 19th, 2014 with Car No.**7033** trailing on a District Line D Stock train about to depart to *Barking*. The station was opened by the LM&SR on September 12th, 1932 and operated from the outset by the UREL District Line. It became part of BR in 1948 and was transferred to London Transport in 1970.

Class 465 EMU No.**465195** at **Woolwich Arsenal station** on May 21st, 2016. It was opened by the South Eastern Railway on December 1st, 1849.

Class 465 EMU No.**465180** exiting from **Plumstead Stabling Point** on May 21st, 2016.

LEGEND
CLOSED LINES
A CUSTOM HOUSE - BECKTON BRANCH
Opened by the Gas Light & Coke Company on October 14th, 1872 to serve Beckton Gas Works, the line closed to passengers on December 29th, 1940 and totally on February 22nd, 1971.

B CUSTOM HOUSE - GALLIONS BRANCH
Opened by the London & St Katherine Dock Company in 1880, closed to passengers on September 9th, 1940 and totally on April 17th, 1966.

MAP 28
1921

A Piccadilly Line train at **Ickenham tube station** on an unknown date. It was opened by the Metropolitan Railway on September 25th, 1905 as *Ickenham Halt* and rebuilt as a station and renamed as *Ickenham* during the 1930s.
J Joyce/Online Transport Archive

Ticket issued by London Transport in the 1970s. **Ruislip Gardens station** was opened by the GWR on July 9th, 1934 and a tube station was subsequently constructed alongside and opened by the LTE on November 21st, 1948. The main line station closed on July 21st, 1958 and was later demolished.

A T Stock train bound for Baker Street, pictured at **Northwood Hills tube station** on an unknown date. The station was opened by the Metropolitan & Great Central Joint Railway on November 13th, 1933 and the T stock was introduced in 1927, remaining in service until October 5th, 1962. *Marcus Eavis/Online Transport*

Looking east at **West Ruislip station** on July 6th, 1974.
Alan Young

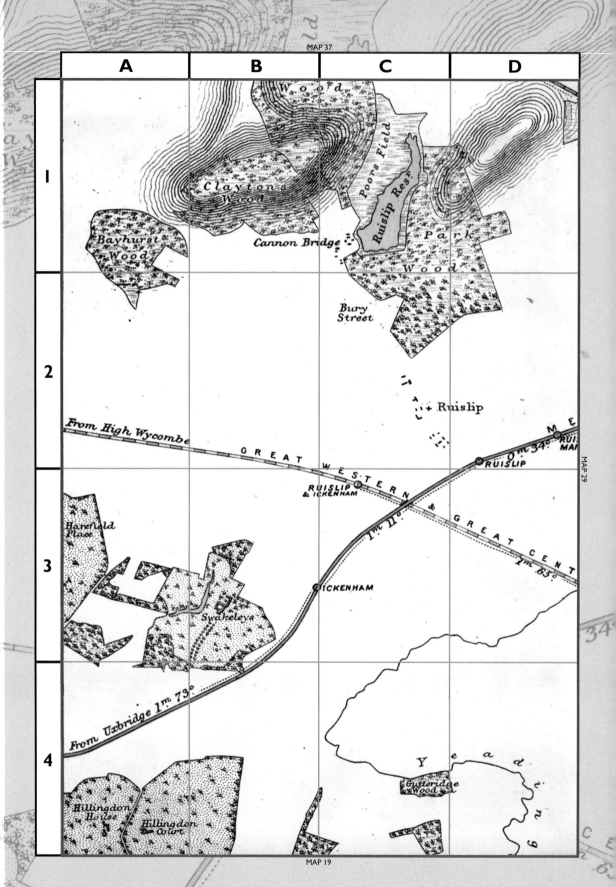

MAP 37

MAP 29

MAP 19

	A	**B**	**C**	**D**	

NORTHWOOD HILLS

RUISLIP MANOR

RUISLIP

WEST RUISLIP

RUISLIP
DEPOT

ICKENHAM

RUISLIP
GARDENS

HILLINGDON [1ST]

HILLINGDON

MAP 29A

MAP 28A
January 1st, 2016

West Ruislip station, looking east, on July 17th, 2016. It was opened jointly by the GWR and GCR on April 2nd, 1906 as *Ruislip & Ickenham*, renamed as *West Ruislip for Ickenham* on June 30th, 1947 and as *West Ruislip* by BR. Stock standing in the adjacent *West Ruislip tube station* can be seen on the right

West Ruislip tube station, looking west, on July 17th, 2016. It was opened by the LPTE on November 21st, 1948.

Ruislip tube station viewed on July 30th, 2016. It was opened by the Harrow & Uxbridge Railway on July 4th, 1904.

Looking north at **Ickenham tube station** on July 30th, 2016. It was opened by the Metropolitan Railway on September 25th, 1905 as *Ickenham Halt* and subsequently renamed as *Ickenham*.

MAP 29
1921

Rayners Lane tube station viewed on on April 4th, 1984.
Alan Young

SIGNAL BOXES

Once a delightful addition to the railway landscape but now, sadly, disappearing rapidly. Here are four examples that come within the remit of this atlas.

Charlton Lane Crossing built by Saxby & Farmer in 1894. *(Map 26)*

Kensington Olympia South Main built in c1880. *(Map 22)*

Greenford East built in 1904 for the GWR. *(Map 21)*

South Tottenham built in 1894 for the GER and still extant. *(Map 33)*

All photographs Cty John Ledward

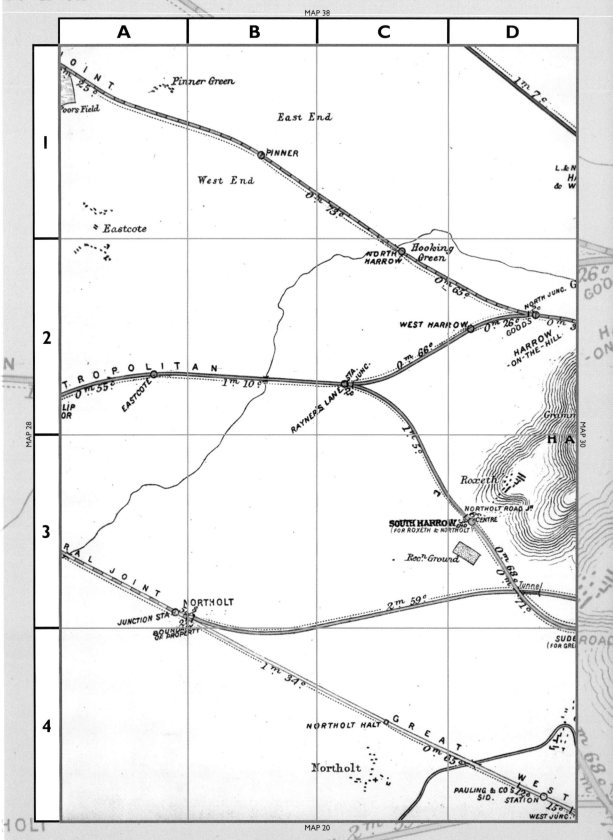

PINNER

MAP 38A

A	B	C	D

PINNER — 1

NORTH HARROW

WEST HARROW — 2

EASTCOTE

RAYNERS
LANE

SOUTH HARROW   SOUTH HARROW [1ST] — 3

NORTHOLT PARK

SOUTH RUISLIP

NORTHOLT HALT

NORTHOLT — 4

GRAND UNION
CANAL

GREENFORD

MAP 28A

MAP 30A

MAP 20A

Looking south at **South Harrow tube station** on March 12th, 2014. The first station here was opened by the District Railway on June 28th, 1903 and was resited a few hundred yards to the north by the LPTB on July 5th, 1935. The original station building, in use as an office for London Underground staff, can be seen on the left of the platform.

Looking west at **Rayners Lane tube station** on July 26th, 2014 with a train of Piccadilly Line 1973 Tube Stock entering the reversing siding. The station was opened by the Metropolitan Railway on May 26th,1906 as *Rayners Lane Halt* and subsequently renamed as *Rayners Lane* in the mid-1930s.

Looking west at **Greenford tube station** on July 17th, 2016. It was opened by the LPTB on June 30th, 1947 as a Central Line station and is also the terminus for the National Rail branch from *West Ealing*. The view above shows the branch line bay platform sandwiched between the two tube platforms.

Pinner tube station viewed on July 9th, 2016. It was opened by the Metropolitan Railway on May 25th, 1885.

MAP 30
1921

Wembley Park (Metropolitan Line) **Depot** viewed on March 3rd, 1991. It was opened in 1932 as a 5-road shed and demolished in 2006. Stabling sidings now occupy the site.
Philip Stuart

The Stanmore branch platform at **Harrow & Wealdstone station** in 1954. The DMU in view was an experimental railcar built by AEC which had been transferred from the St Albans Abbey branch on March 15th, 1954. It was returned during the following year and by this time passenger services only extended to the station at *Belmont*, which had been opened by the LM&SR on September 12th, 1932. *(See Note **A** on Map 30A)*
J Joyce/Online Transport Archive

Sudbury & Harrow Road station on July 2nd, 1973. It was opened by the GCR on March 1st, 1906.
Alan Young

The mainline platforms at **Harrow & Wealdstone station** viewed on March 30th, 1974. It was opened by the London & Birmingham Railway on July 20th, 1837 as *Harrow Weald*, renamed as *Harrow* in the same year and as *Harrow & Wealdstone* by the L&NWR on May 1st, 1897.
Alan Young

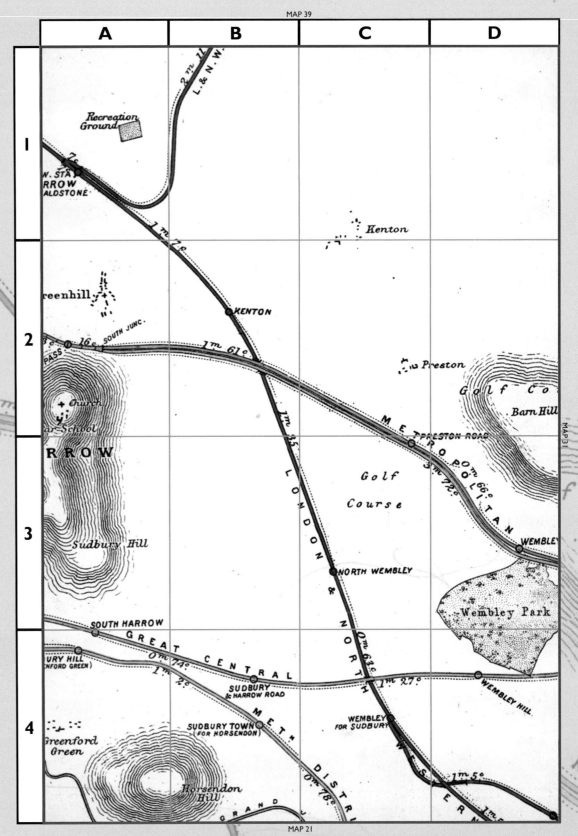

MAP 39A

A	B	C	D

BELMONT

A

QUEENSBURY

1

HARROW & WEALDSTONE

KINGSBURY

KENTON

HARROW-ON-THE-HILL

NORTHWICK PARK

2

PRESTON ROAD

PRESTON ROAD [1ST]

SOUTH KENTON

WEMBLEY PARK

3

NORTH WEMBLEY

B

WEMBLEY STADIUM (LNER)

SUDBURY HILL HARROW

SUDBURY & HARROW ROAD

WEMBLEY STADIUM

SUDBURY HILL

WEMBLEY DEPOT

SUDBURY TOWN

WEMBLEY CENTRAL

4

STONEBRIDGE PARK DEPOT

STONEBRIDGE PARK DEPOT

GRAND UNION CANAL

STONEBRIDGE PARK

MAP 21A

SUDBURY & HARROW ROAD

MAP 29A

MAP 31A

A Jubilee Line 1996 Tube Stock train, with Car No. **96042** leading, at **Wembley Park tube station**, on March 12th, 2014. The station was opened by the Metropolitan Railway on May 12th, 1894.

Looking north at **Kenton station** on July 26th, 2014 with Car No.3244 leading a train of 1972 Mark II Stock on a Bakerloo Line service. It was opened by the L&NWR on June 15th, 1912, renamed as *Kenton for Northwick Park* by the LMSR in 1927 and reverted back to *Kenton* by BR in 1973.

Stonebridge Park station, looking south, on June 4th, 2016. It was opened by the L&NWR on June 15th, 1912, closed on January 9th, 1917 and reopened on August 1st, 1917.

LEGEND
CLOSED LINES

A STANMORE VILLAGE BRANCH
Opened by the L&NWR on December 18th, 1890, passenger services between Belmont and Stanmore Village were withdrawn by BR on September 15th, 1952 and freight services ceased on July 6th, 1964. Passenger services between Belmont and Harrow & Wealdstone were finally withdrawn on October 5th, 1964.

B WEMBLEY STADIUM LOOP
Opened by the LNER on April 28th, 1923 to serve the Empire Exhibition at Wembley Stadium and closed by BR on May 18th, 1968.

WEMBLEY STADIUM

MAP 31
1921

Cricklewood MPD on July 16th, 1967. It was opened by the MR in 1882 as a single roundhouse and was originally known as *Childs Hill*. A second roundhouse was added in 1893 and the depot was closed to steam by BR on December 14th, 1964. It continued in use for a few years as a diesel stabling and servicing point.
WT Stubbs

Ex-Metropolitan Railway E Class 0-4-4T No.L48 at **Willesden Green tube station** on a *Railway World Special* on May 23rd, 1954. The locomotive was built by Hawthorn Leslie in 1901 as MET No.81 and the station was opened by the Metropolitan Railway on November 24th, 1879. It was renamed as *Willesden Green & Cricklewood* on June 1st, 1894 and reverted back to the original name by the LPTB in 1938.
J Joyce/Online Transport Archive

Neasden MPD was opened by the GCR on March 15th, 1899 and closed by BR on June 18th, 1962. The view above shows a busy shed yard on September 20th, 1959.
WT Stubbs

LEGEND
I LINE UNDER CONSTRUCTION

Golders Green to Edgware
This line was built by the Charing Cross, Euston & Hampstead Railway. The first section, from Golders Green to Hendon Central, opened on November 19th, 1923 and the line reached Edgware on August 18th, 1924.

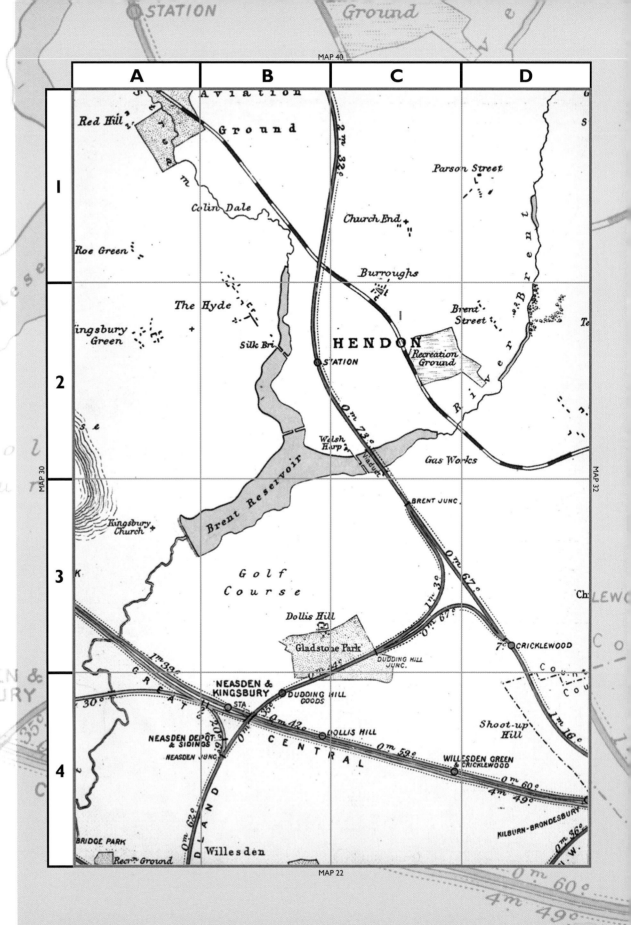

Map Grid

	A	B	C	D
1	BURNT OAK	COLINDALE		
2		HENDON	HENDON CENTRAL, BRENT CROSS	RIVER BRENT
3	BRENT RESERVOIR			CRICKLEWOOD
4	A, NEASDEN DEPOT, NEASDEN	DOLLIS HILL	WILLESDEN GREEN, KILBURN	

MAP 40A

MAP 30A

MAP 32A

MAP 22A

NEASDEN DEPOT

Looking west at **Dollis Hill tube station** on July 9th, 2016. It was opened by the Metropolitan Railway on October 1st, 1909 as *Dollis Hill*, renamed as *Dollis Hill & Gladstone Park* in 1931 and reverted back to *Dollis Hill* in 1933.

Looking west at **Neasden tube station** on July 9th, 2016. It was opened by the Kingsbury & Harrow Railway on August 2nd, 1880 as *Kingsbury & Neasden*, renamed as *Neasden & Kingsbury* by the Metropolitan Railway on January 1st, 1910 and as *Neasden* on January 1st, 1932.

Class 319 EMU No.319217 at **Cricklewood station** on July 16th, 2016 with a service to *St Albans City*. The station was opened by the MR on May 2nd, 1870 as *Child's Hill & Cricklewood* and renamed as *Cricklewood* on May 1st, 1903.

LEGEND
CLOSED LINES
A WEMBLEY STADIUM LOOP
Opened by the LNER on April 28th, 1923 to serve the Empire Exhibition at Wembley Stadium and closed by BR on May 18th, 1968.

MAP 32
1921

Highgate (Northern Line) **Depot**, looking north on December 22nd, 1990. *Philip Stuart*

Finchley Road tube station was opened by the Metropolitan Railway on June 30th, 1879, renamed as *Finchley Road (South Hampstead)* in 1885 and reverted back to *Finchley Road* in 1917. This Platform Ticket was issued on January 7th, 1957.

Kentish Town station on May 11th, 1973. It was opened by the MR on July 13th, 1868. *Alan Young*

Golders Green tube station on March 11th, 1956. It was opened by the Charing Cross, Euston & Hampstead Railway on June 22nd, 1907.
Marcus Eavis/Online Transport Archive

LEGEND
1 LINE UNDER CONSTRUCTION

Golders Green to Edgware
This line was built by the Charing Cross, Euston & Hampstead Railway. The first section, from Golders Green to Hendon Central, opened on November 19th, 1923 and the line reached Edgware on August 18th, 1924.

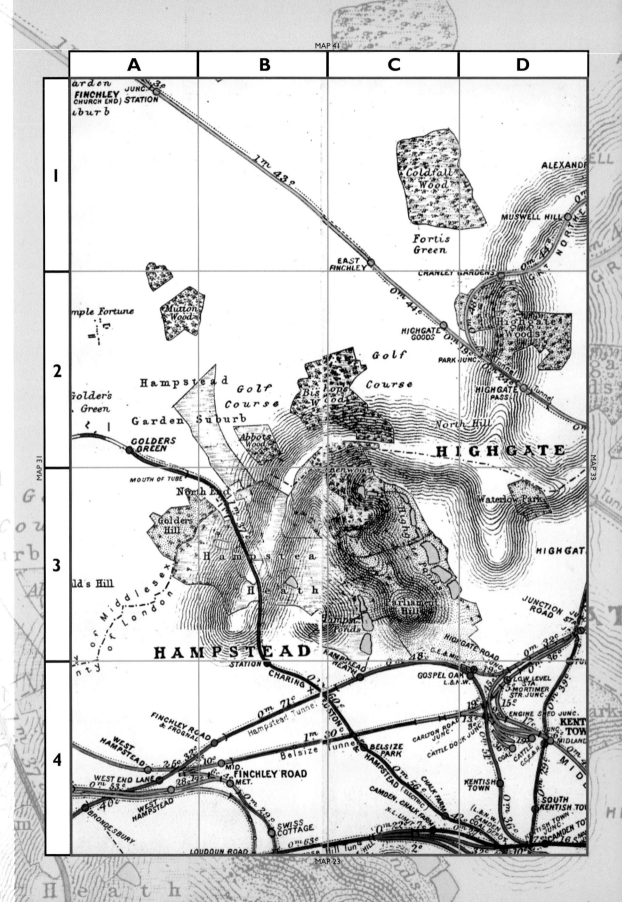

MAP 41A

A	B	C	D

FINCHLEY CENTRAL

1

MUSWELL HILL

EAST FINCHLEY

A

HIGHGATE
DEPOT

CRANLEY GARDENS

2

B

HIGHGATE

GOLDERS GREEN
DEPOT

GOLDERS
GREEN

MAP 31A

MAP 33A

3

JUNCTION ROAD

HIGHGATE ROAD
LOW LEVEL

TUFNELL
PARK

HAMPSTEAD

GOSPEL
OAK

HAMPSTEAD
HEATH

FINCHLEY ROAD
& FROGNAL

KENTISH
TOWN

WEST
HAMPSTEAD
THAMESLINK

FINCHLEY ROAD

BELSIZE PARK

KENTISH
TOWN

4

WEST
HAMPSTEAD

FINCHLEY ROAD

KENTISH TOWN WEST

WEST
HAMPSTEAD

CHALK
FARM

SOUTH
KENTISH
TOWN

BRONDESBURY

SWISS COTTAGE

CHALK FARM

CAMDEN
ROAD

MAP 23A

FINCHLEY ROAD

Finchley Central tube station on April 5th, 2014 with 1995 Tube Stock cars Nos **51634** and **51525** in view. The station was built by the Edgware, Highgate & London Railway in 1867 but, before the line was completed, it was purchased by the GNR and opened on August 22nd, 1867 as *Finchley & Hendon*. It was renamed as *Finchley* on February 1st, 1872, as *Finchley (Church End)* on February 1st 1894 and as *Finchley Central* by the L&NER on April 1st, 1940.

Northern Line services started using the station from April 14th, 1940, the L&NER ceased using it in the following year and the LPTB subsequently assumed responsibility for the station.

Hampstead Heath station, looking west, on June 4th, 2016. It was opened by the Hampstead Junction Railway on January 2nd, 1860 and closed between December 4th, 1984 and April 15th, 1985 due to the collapse of a retaining wall.

LEGEND
CLOSED LINES

A ALEXANDRA PALACE BRANCH
The line was opened from Highgate by the Edgware, Highgate & London and Muswell Hill & Palace railways on May 24th, 1873 and worked from the outset by the GNR. It was subsequently taken over by the LPTB and was due to be electrified as part of the Northern Line but post war economies forced the cancellation of the project and the line closed to passengers by BR on July 5th, 1954 and totally on May 18th, 1957. Part of the route is now the Parkland Walk.

B FINSBURY PARK – HIGHGATE LINE
Opened by the Edgware, Highgate & London Railway on August 22nd, 1867 as part of the Finsbury Park to Edgware and Alexandra Palace lines and worked from the outset by the GNR, it was subsequently taken over the by LPTB and was due to be electrified as part of the Northern Line but post-war economies forced the cancellation of the project. Passenger services ceased on July 5th, 1954 and the line was retained for freight and Northern Line stock movements until October 5th, 1970. The track was lifted in 1972 and part of the route is now the Parkland Walk.

MAP 33
1921

Hornsey MPD viewed on September 20th, 1959. It was opened by the GNR in 1899 and, since 1958 had become the first depot at the London end of the East Coast Main Line to service diesels. It was officially closed to steam in June 1961 and served as a diesel depot for the next ten years. It currently forms part of Hornsey EMU depot. *WT Stubbs*

A train approaching **Dalston Junction** at an unknown date. The station was opened by the North London Railway on November 1st, 1865, closed by BR on June 30th, 1986 and reopened by London Overground on April 27th, 2010. *Marcus Eavis/Online Transport Archive*

A derelict and line-lifted **Alexandra Palace station** on July 25th, 1956. The short branch from Highgate, along with the station was opened by the Muswell Hill Railway on May 24th, 1873. During its existence it suffered from poor patronage and opened and closed on numerous occasions until finally closed by BR on July 5th, 1954. *Marcus Eavis/Online Transport Archive*

A	B	C	D

PALACE GATES WOOD GREEN

WOOD GREEN

ALEXANDRA PALACE

ALEXANDRA PALACE

A

NOEL PARK & WOOD GREEN

C

BRUCE GROVE

1

TURNPIKE LANE

WEST GREEN

HORNSEY

HORNSEY DEPOT

SEVEN SISTERS

ST ANN'S ROAD

HARRINGAY GREEN LANES

SOUTH TOTTENHAM

2

HARRINGAY

CROUCH END

STROUD GREEN

NEW RIVER

STAMFORD HILL

B

CROUCH HILL

MANOR HOUSE

EAST RESERVOIR

HORNSEY ROAD

WEST RESERVOIR

ARCHWAY

STOKE NEWINGTON

FINSBURY PARK   FINSBURY PARK

3

UPPER HOLLOWAY

ARSENAL

HOLLOWAY ROAD

DRAYTON PARK

CALEDONIAN ROAD

MILDMAY PARK

DALSTON KINGSLAND

CANONBURY

HIGHBURY & ISLINGTON

CALEDONIAN ROAD & BARNSBURY

4

MAIDEN LANE

DALSTON JUNCTION

MAP 33A
January 1st, 2016

The former station building at **Alexandra Palace** on March 3rd, 2016, now in use as a community centre. A car park occupies the site of the platforms and track.

Class 378 EMU No.378221 at **Canonbury station**, on June 4th, 2016. It was opened by the North London Railway on December 1st, 1870, replacing a station that had opened on September 1st, 1858 and was sited due east.

LEGEND
CLOSED LINES

A ALEXANDRA PALACE BRANCH
The line was opened from Highgate by the Edgware, Highgate & London and Muswell Hill & Palace railways on May 24th, 1873 and worked from the outset by the GNR. It was subsequently taken over by the LPTB and was due to be electrified as part of the Northern Line but post war economies forced the cancellation of the project and the line closed to passengers by BR on July 5th, 1954 and totally on May 18th, 1957. Part of the route is now the Parkland Walk.

B FINSBURY PARK – HIGHGATE LINE
Opened by the Edgware, Highgate & London Railway on August 22nd, 1867 as part of the Finsbury Park to Edgware and Alexandra Palace lines and worked from the outset by the GNR, it was subsequently taken over the by LPTB and was due to be electrified as part of the Northern Line but post war economies forced the cancellation of the project. Passenger services ceased on July 5th, 1954 and the line was retained for freight and Northern Line stock movements until October 5th, 1970. The track was lifted in 1972 and part of the route is now the Parkland Walk.

C PALACE GATES BRANCH
Opened by GER on January 1st, 1878, closed to passengers by BR on January 7th, 1963 and totally on February 7th, 1965.

MAP 43

MAP 34
1921

Wood Street, Walthamstow MPD viewed on April 2nd, 1960 the year of closure. It was opened by the GER in 1897.

A local train entering **Hackney Downs station** on April 22nd, 1956. The station was opened by the GER on May 27th, 1872 as *Hackney Downs Junction* and renamed as *Hackney Downs* in 1896.
Marcus Eavis/Online Transport Archive

Looking east at **St James Street, Walthamstow station** on May 23rd, 1973. It was opened by the GER on April 26th, 1870.   *Alan Young*

Lea Bridge station viewed on July 25th, 1975. It was opened by Northern & Eastern Railway on September 15th, 1840 as *Lea Bridge Road*, renamed as *Lea Bridge* by the GER in April 1871 and closed by BR on July 8th, 1985. It was reopened on May 15th, 2016. *Alan Young*

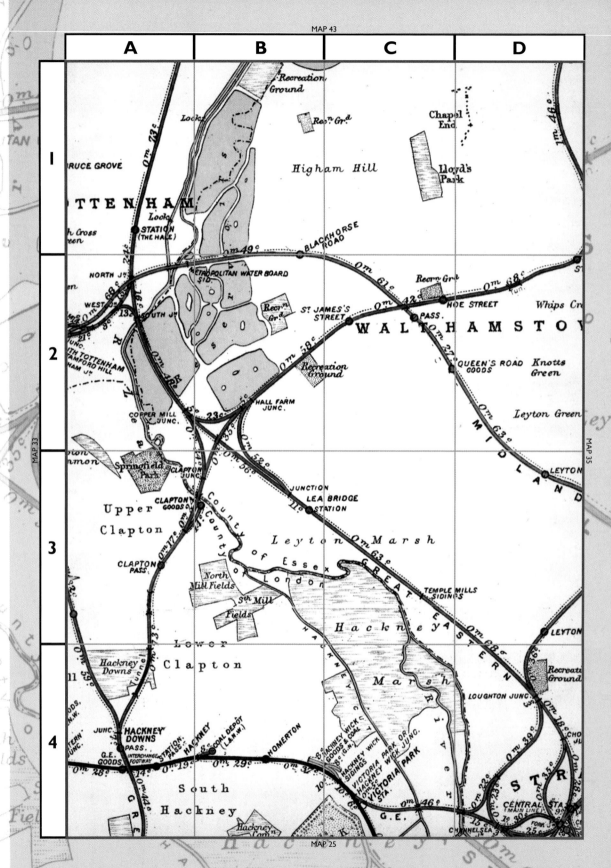

MAP 25

MAP 43A

| A | B | C | D |

NORTHUMBERLAND
PARK DEPOT

LOCKWOOD
RESERVOIR

TEN
HALE

1

TOTTENHAM
HALE

WOOD STREET

BLACKHORSE
ROAD

WALTHAMSTOW
CENTRAL

ST JAMES STREET
WALTHAMSTOW

WALTHAMSTOW QUEEN'S ROAD

WARWICK
RESERVOIR

2

MAP 33A

LEYTON MIDLAND ROAD

LEA BRIDGE

TEMPLE MILLS
EUROSTAR
DEPOT

3

CLAPTON

RECTORY
ROAD

HACKNEY
CUT

LEYTON

RIVER LEE

STRATFORD
INTERNATIONAL

HACKNEY
DOWNS

HACKNEY
CENTRAL

HOMERTON

4

VICTORIA PARK

HACKNEY WICK

STRATFORD†

A

MAP 25A

Class 66 Diesel Electric Locomotive No.**66772** passing through **Hackney Wick station** on June 4th, 2016. The station was opened by BR on May 12th, 1980.

Stratford International station, looking east, on June 4th, 2016. Although completed by April 2006 it was not opened until November 30th, 2009.

Stratford International DLR station on June 4th, 2016 with B92 Stock Train No.**89** about to depart to *Woolwich Arsenal*. The station was opened on August 31st, 2011.

STATIONS
† **STRATFORD** station managed by **Transport for London** from May 2015

LEGEND
CLOSED LINES
A VICTORIA PARK – BOW
Opened by the North London Railway on September 26th, 1850 and closed to passengers during World War 2 on May 15th, 1944 the line was totally closed by BR on October 3rd, 1983.

MAP 35
1921

MAP 44

A BR ticket issued for the short journey between *Leyton (Midland Road)* and **Leytonstone (High Road)**. Both stations were opened by the Tottenham & Forest Gate Joint Railway on July 9th, 1894, the former as *Leyton* and the latter as *Leytonstone* and both were renamed, to those on the ticket, by BR on May 1st, 1949.

Manor Park station viewed on May 30th, 1974. It was also opened by the GER on January 6th, 1873 and was also described as *Manor Park for Little Ilford* in some timetables. *Alan Young*

Forest Gate station on May 30th, 1974. It was opened by the Eastern Counties Railway in 1840, closed on June 1st, 1843 and reopened on May 31st, 1846. It was also described as *Forest Gate for Upton* in some timetables. *Alan Young*

Maryland station on March 18th, 1979. It was opened by the GER on January 6th, 1873 as *Maryland Point* and renamed as *Maryland* by the L&NER on October 28th, 1940. *Alan Young*

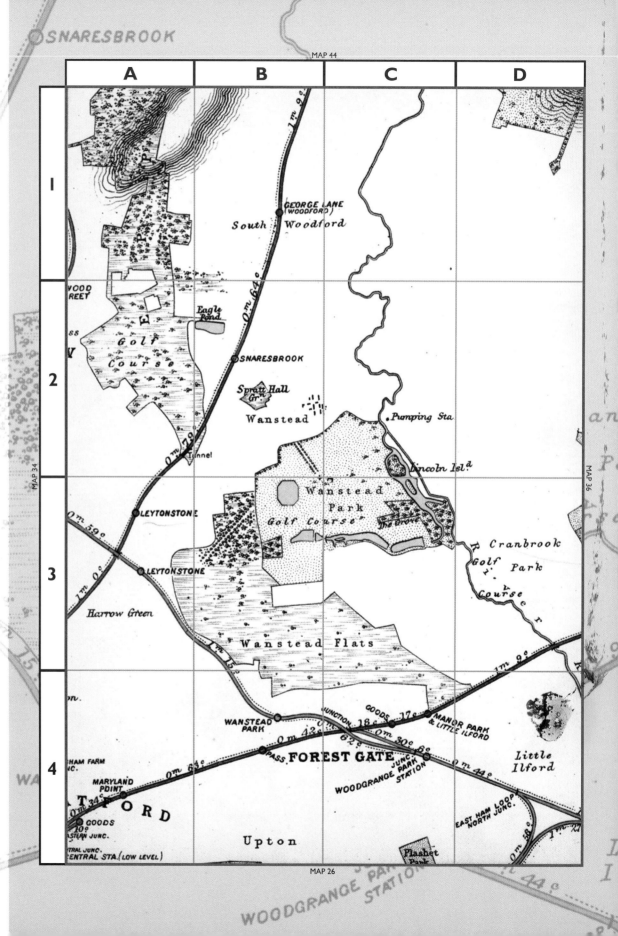

MAP 44A

	A	B	C	D	

MAP 34A

MAP 36A

1

RIVER
RODING

SOUTH WOODFORD

2

SNARESBROOK

WANSTEAD

REDBRIDGE

LEYTONSTONE

LEYTONSTONE
HIGH ROAD

3

RIVER
RODING

WANSTEAD
PARK

MANOR
PARK†

FOREST GATE†

WOODGRANGE PARK

MARYLAND†

EAST
HAM
DEPOT

4

MAP 26A

RYLAND

ONST

MAN

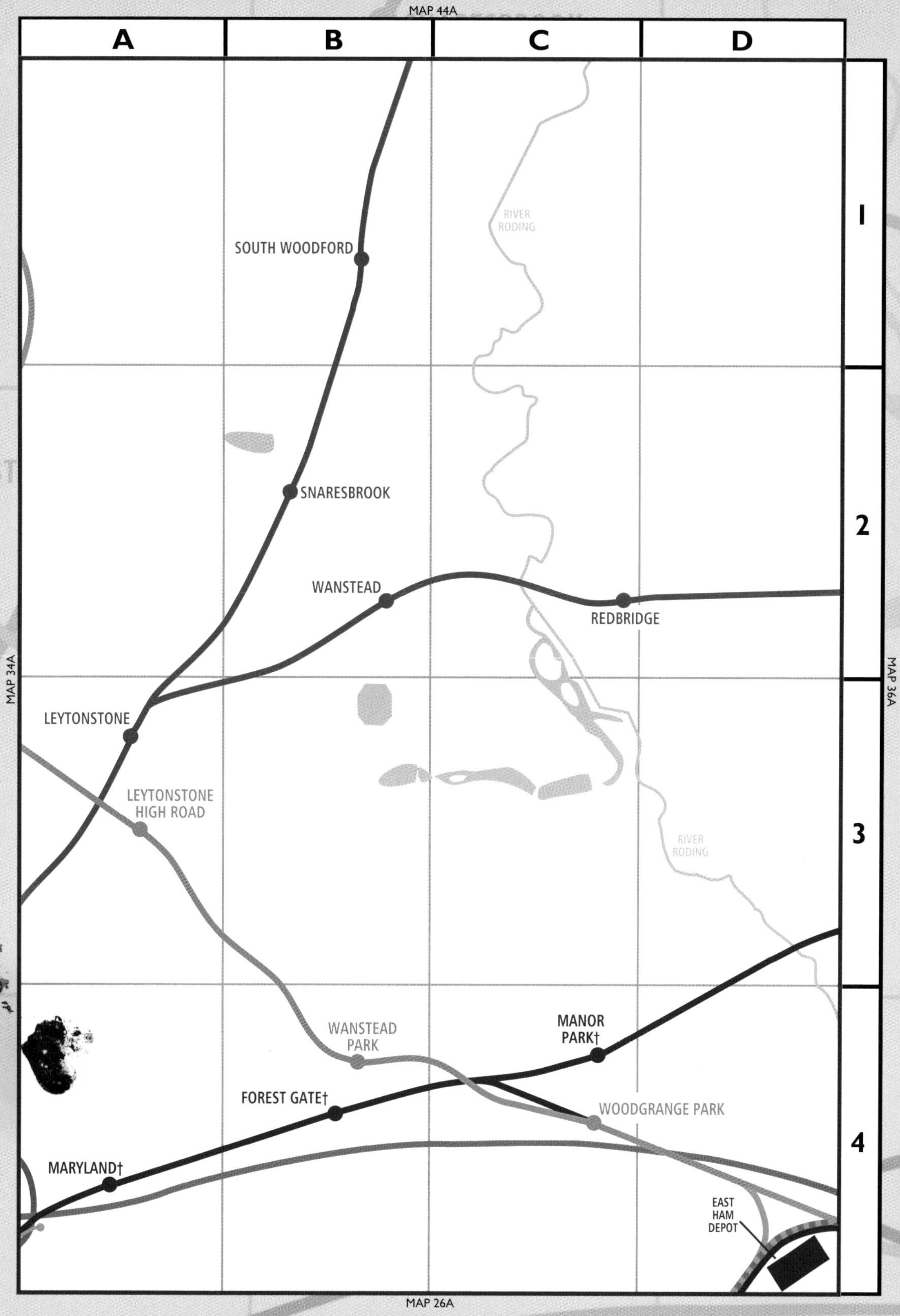

A 1992 Tube stock train, with car No.91171 leading, at **Leytonstone tube station** on July 9th, 2016. It was opened by the Eastern Counties Railway on August 22nd, 1856.

Snaresbrook tube station, looking north, on July 9th, 2016. It was opened by the Eastern Counties Railway on August 22nd, 1856 as *Snaresbrook*, renamed as *Snaresbrook for Wanstead* in 1857, as *Snaresbrook & Wanstead* by the GER in November 1898, as *Snaresbrook for Wanstead* by the L&NER in 1929 and as *Snaresbrook* on December 14th, 1947.

Manor Park station, looking east, on July 16th, 2016. It was opened by the GER on January 6th, 1873 and was referred to as *Manor Park for Little Ilford* in some timetables.

STATIONS
† MARYLAND, FOREST GATE and MANOR PARK stations managed by **Transport for London** from May 2015.

MAP 45

MAP 36
1921

Ilford Shed viewed on January 30th, 1938 with Class J15 0-6-0 No.7901 and Class N7 0-6-0T Nos 2625 and 2624 on the shed road. It was opened by the GER in 1901 and closed by the LNER in May 1939.
WA Camwell

Fairlop tube station viewed on June 18th, 1986.
Alan Young

Looking east at **Seven Kings station** on May 30th, 1974. The station was opened by the GER on March 1st, 1899.
Alan Young

Ilford station viewed on May 30th, 1974. The station was opened by the Eastern Counties Railway on June 20th, 1839.
Alan Young

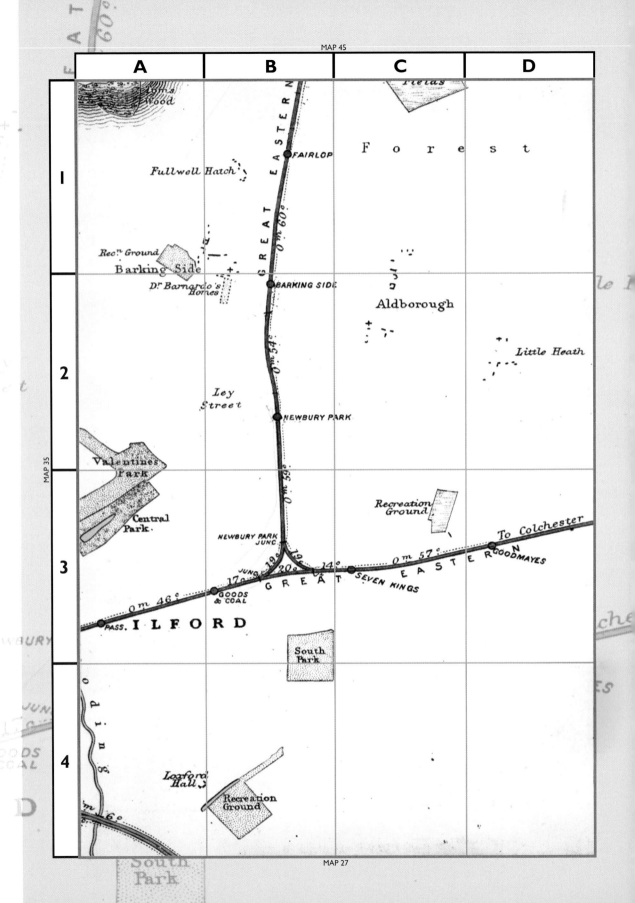

MAP 27

A	B	C	D

FAIRLOP

BARKINGSIDE

GANTS HILL

NEWBURY PARK

A

ILFORD
DEPOT

GOODMAYES†

SEVEN KINGS†

ILFORD†

MAP 35A

HILL

RIVER
RODING

MAP 27A

SEVEN KINGS

I

2

3

4

The entrance to **Barkingside tube station** on July 9th, 2016. The Grade II listed station was opened by the GER on May 1st, 1903 as *Barking Side*, subsequently renamed as *Barkingside*, closed on May 22nd, 1916 and reopened on July 1st, 1919.

Looking south at **Fairlop tube station** on July 9th, 2016. The station was opened by the GER on May 1st, 1903.

Goodmayes station viewed on July 16th, 2016. The station was opened by the GER on February 8th, 1901.

STATIONS
† ILFORD, SEVEN KINGS and GOODMAYES stations managed by **Transport for London** from May 2015

LEGEND
CLOSED LINES
A NEWBURY PARK – ILFORD
Opened by GER on April 20th, 1903 and closed to passengers by the LNER on November 30th, 1947. The western curve was also closed to freight but the eastern curve was retained until the whole line was closed by BR on March 19th, 1956.

GOODMAYES

MAP 37
1921

Ex-Metropolitan Railway Bo-Bo Electric Locomotive No.18 *Michael Faraday* at **Rickmansworth** on May 23rd, 1954. The locomotive was withdrawn in 1962 and scrapped in 1966. The station was opened by the Metropolitan Railway on September 1st, 1887 and became the changeover point from electric traction to steam on the Aylesbury and Chesham lines. A stabling and servicing point for steam locomotives was established here by the L&NER/Metropolitan Railway on January 25th, 1925 and closed by BR on September 9th, 1961.   *J Joyce/Online Transport Archive*

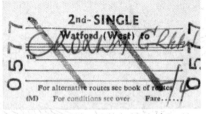

Two BR-era tickets *(above and below)* issued for services on the now-closed Croxley Green branch. Both *Croxley Green* and *Watford North* stations effectively closed on March 25th, 1996 when a new road was built across the line. *(See Note **B** in Legend on Map 37A)*

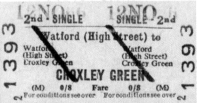

Croxley Green station on June 19th, 1986. It was opened by the L&NWR on June 15th, 1912.

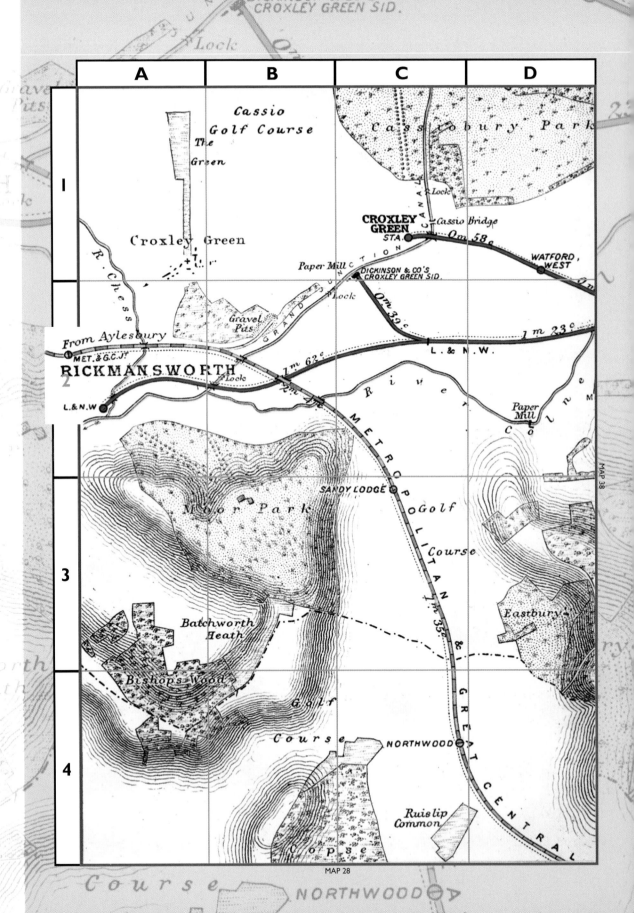

	A	B	C	D	

WATFORD

CROXLEY
GREEN

B

GRAND UNION
CANAL

WATFORD
WEST

CROXLEY

RIVER
CHESS

A

RICKMANSWORTH

RIVER
COLNE

RICKMANSWORTH
(CHURCH STREET)

MOOR PARK

NORTHWOOD

I

2

3

4

MAP 38A

MAP 28A

Rickmansworth station on May 3rd, 2014 with S Stock car No.**21004** leading on an eastbound train. The station was opened by the Metropolitan (Harrow & Rickmansworth) Railway on September 1st, 1887 and until September 9th, 1961 was the changeover point from steam to electric locomotives on Metropolitan Line services from Amersham and Verney Junction.

An S8 Stock train, with car No.**21095** trailing, about to depart from **Moor Park tube station** on a service to Chesham on May 3rd, 2014. The station was opened by the Metropolitan and Great Central railways as *Sandy Lodge* on May 9th, 1910, renamed as *Moor Park & Sandy Lodge* on October 18th, 1923 and as *Moor Park* on September 25th, 1950.

LEGEND
CLOSED LINES
A RICKMANSWORTH (CHURCH STREET) BRANCH

Opened by the Watford & Rickmansworth Railway from Watford Junction on October 1st, 1862, closed to passengers by BR on March 3rd, 1952 and completely on January 2nd, 1967.

B CROXLEY GREEN BRANCH

The branch was opened by the L&NWR on June 15th, 1912 and, although never officially closed, passenger services were suspended from March 25th, 1996 when a new road was built across the route. In 2014 the trackbed was scheduled for part of the route of a new Metropolitan Line linking the existing Watford line to Watford Junction via Watford High Street, and this is due to open in 2020.

MAP 38
1921

Ex-LMS Class 4 2-6-4T No.**42096** in the shed yard at **Watford MPD** on March 8th, 1964. It was opened the L&NWR in 1872 and closed by BR on March 29th, 1965. The shed was demolished and the site is now in use as the station car park.   *KCH Fairey*

Bushey station viewed on March 30th, 1974. It was opened the L&NWR on December 1st, 1841, renamed as *Bushey & Oxhey* on December 1st, 1912 and reverted back to *Bushey* by BR on May 6th, 1974.   *Alan Young*

Looking north at **Carpenders Park station** on March 30th, 1974.   *Alan Young*

Hatch End station viewed on March 30th, 1974. It was opened by the London & Birmingham Railway in 1844 as *Pinner*, renamed as *Pinner & Hatch End* by the L&NWR on January 1st, 1897, as *Hatch End for Pinner* on February 1st, 1920 and as *Hatch End* by BR on June 11th, 1956.   *Alan Young*

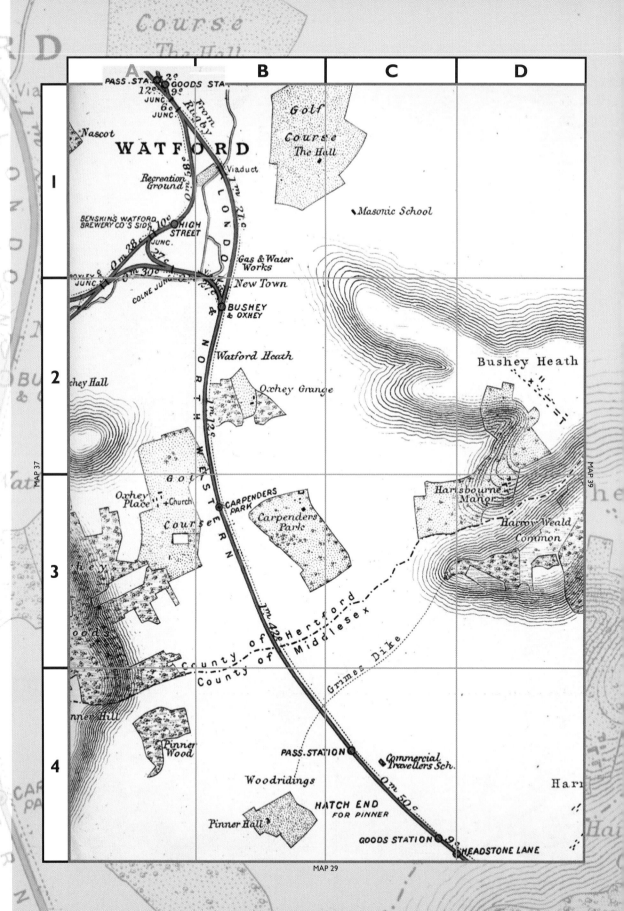

A WATFORD JUNCTION

B

C

D

WATFORD HIGH STREET

RIVER COLNE

BUSHEY

B

A

CARPENDERS PARK

HATCH END

HEADSTONE LANE

1

2

3

4

MAP 37A

MAP 39A

MAP 29A

Watford High Street station, looking north, on May 26th, 2016. It was opened by the L&NWR on October 1st, 1862 and is due to also become a Metropolitan Line tube station in 2020 *(See note **B** below)*.

Carpenders Park station, looking north, on May 26th, 2016. It was opened by BR on November 17th, 1952, replacing the former L&NWR station sited some 230 yards to the north.

Looking north at **Headstone Lane station** on August 6th, 2016. It was opened by the L&NWR on February 10th, 1913.

LEGEND
CLOSED LINES

A RICKMANSWORTH (CHURCH STREET) BRANCH

Opened by the Watford & Rickmansworth Railway from Watford Junction on October 1st, 1862, closed to passengers by BR on March 3rd, 1952 and completely on January 2nd, 1967.

B CROXLEY GREEN BRANCH

The branch was opened by the LNWR on June 15th, 1912 and, although never officially closed, passenger services were suspended from March 25th, 1996 when a new road was built across the route. In 2014 the trackbed was scheduled for part of the route of a new Metropolitan Line linking the existing Watford line to Watford Junction via Watford High Street, and this is due to open in 2020.

MAP 39
1921

Edgware (Northern Line) tube station and **depot** viewed on December 1st, 1990. The station was opened on August 18th, 1924 as the terminus of the second phase of construction from Golders Green. It had been intended to continue to Bushey Heath but this was not undertaken. The depot was also opened in 1924.   *Philip Stuart*

Edgware station viewed on an unrecorded date after closure. It was opened by the GNR (Edgware, Highgate & London Railway) on August 22nd, 1867 and closed to passengers by the L&NER on September 11th, 1939. A one-road engine shed was also erected here, opening on the same day as the station and closing in July 1878. *(See note B on Map 39A).*   *Alan Young Collection*

Stanmore Village station viewed in 1957. It was opened by the L&NWR (Harrow & Stanmore Railway) on December 18th, 1890 as *Stanmore*, renamed as *Stanmore Village* by BR on September 25th, 1950 and closed on September 15th, 1952. *(See note A on Map 39A)*   *Alan Young Collection*

LEGEND
I LINE UNDER CONSTRUCTION

Golders Green to Edgware
This line was built by the Charing Cross, Euston & Hampstead Railway. The first section, from Golders Green to Hendon Central, opened on November 19th, 1923 and the line reached Edgware on August 18th, 1924.

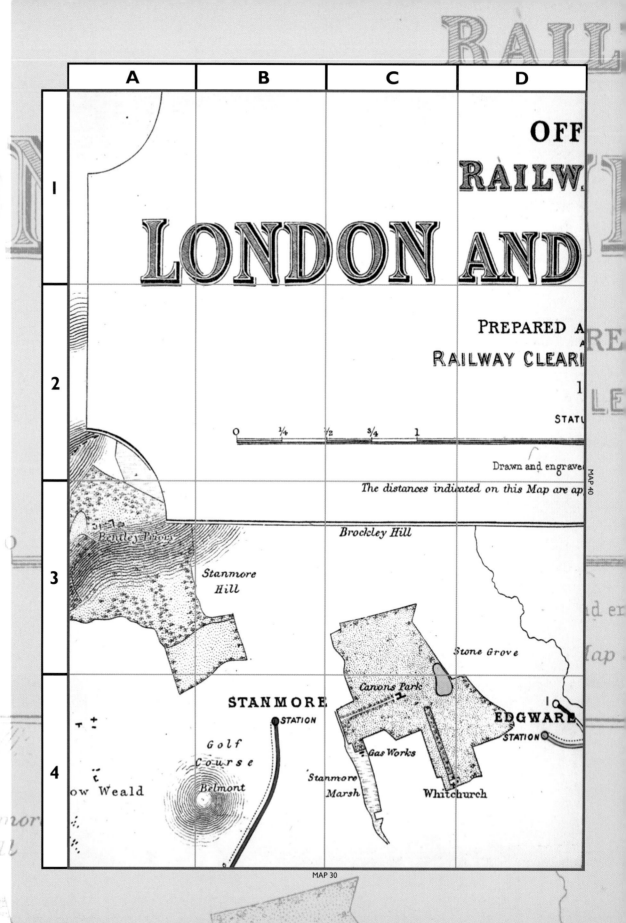

	A	B	C	D	
1					
2					
3					
4					

MAP 38A

MAP 40A

ELSTREE & BOREHAMWOOD

STANMORE

STANMORE VILLAGE

EDGWARE DEPOT

EDGWARE

EDGWARE (GNR)

CANONS PARK

A

B

MAP 30A

CANONS PARK

The entrance to the Stanley Heaps-designed **Edgware tube station**, viewed on April 2nd, 2016.

Looking south at **Elstree & Borehamwood station** on July 9th, 2016. It was opened by the MR on July 13th, 1868 as *Elstree* and renamed as *Elstree & Boreham Wood* on June 1st, 1869, as *Elstree* on April 1st, 1904, as *Elstree & Borehamwood* by BR on September 1st, 1953, as *Elstree* on May 6th, 1974 and finally as *Elstree & Borehamwood* on May 5th, 1988.

Stanmore Tube station viewed on July 9th, 2016. It was opened by the Metropolitan Railway on December 10th, 1932.

LEGEND
CLOSED LINES
A STANMORE VILLAGE BRANCH
Opened by the L&NWR on December 18th, 1890, passenger services between Belmont and Stanmore Village were withdrawn by BR on September 15th, 1952 and freight services ceased on July 6th, 1964. Passenger services between Belmont and Harrow & Wealdstone were finally withdrawn on October 5th, 1964.

B EDGWARE (GNR) BRANCH
Opened from Finchley Central by the GNR on August 22nd, 1867 and subsequently taken over by the LPTB, it was due to be electrified as part of the Northern Line. Passenger services ceased shortly after the start of World War 2 on September 11th, 1939 but post war economies forced the cancellation of the project and the line west of Mill Hill East, which had been retained for freight, closed on June 1st, 1964 and was abandoned. Part of the route is now the Parkland Walk.

MAP 40
1921

A Northern Line train at **Mill Hill East tube station** on an unrecorded date *(see note A on Map 40A).*
J Joyce/Online Transport Archive

LONDON TRANSPORT
Issued subject to the Bye-Laws, Regulations and Conditions of L.T. Board. Available day of issue only.

MILL HILL (THE HALE)

any one of L.T. stations shown on Fares list at a SINGLE FARE of
Mill Hill (The Hale) Mill Hill (The Hale)
2/9 **2/9** **2/9**

Mill Hill (The Hale) station was opened by the GNR on June 11th, 1906 as *The Hale Halt*, renamed as *The Hale for Mill Hill* in May 1912 and as *Mill Hill (The Hale)** by the LNER on March 1st, 1928. It was temporarily closed on September 11th, 1939 in preparation for the LPTB to take over *(See note A on Map 40A)* but never reopened.

After World War 2, despite the non-existence of the station, London Transport issued tickets for *Mill Hill (The Hale)* to enable passengers to alight at *Mill Hill East* and board a No.240A 'bus for any destination along the route to Edgware.
* Some sources quote the name as *Mill Hill for The Hale*

Ex-LMS Class 4 2-6-4T No.**42595** standing at **Mill Hill Broadway station** in 1957.
Bob Collier - Alan Young Collection

LEGEND
I LINE UNDER CONSTRUCTION

Golders Green to Edgware
This line was built by the Charing Cross, Euston & Hampstead Railway. The first section, from Golders Green to Hendon Central, opened on November 19th, 1923 and the line reached Edgware on August 18th, 1924.

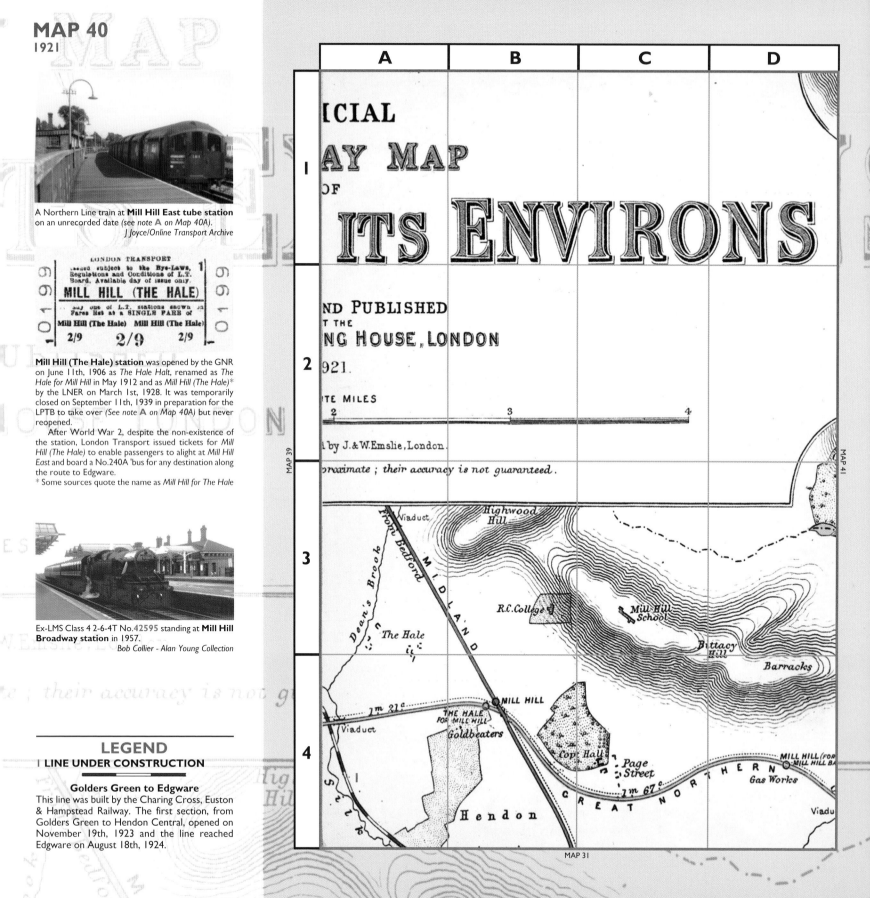

	A	B	C	D
1				
2				
3				
4				

MAP 39A

MAP 41A

MAP 31A

MILL HILL BROADWAY

MILL HILL
(THE HALE)

MILL HILL
EAST

A

Mill Hill East tube station on April 2nd, 2016, looking west towards the buffer stops and abandoned trackbed beyond

Class 319 EMU No.319007 at **Mill Hill Broadway station** on April 2nd, 2016. It was opened by the Midland Railway on July 13th, 1868 as *Mill Hill* and renamed as *Mill Hill Broadway* by BR on September 25th, 1950.

The main entrance to **Mill Hill Broadway station** on April 2nd, 2016. In 1966 the M1 was constructed adjacent to the east side of the line and the station was rebuilt to accommodate this, resulting in the main buildings being sited under the northbound carriageway of the motorway.

LEGEND
CLOSED LINES
A EDGWARE (GNR) BRANCH
Opened from Finchley Central by the GNR on August 22nd, 1867 and subsequently taken over by the LPTB, it was due to be electrified as part of the Northern Line. Passenger services ceased shortly after the start of World War 2 on September 11th, 1939 but post war economies forced the cancellation of the project and the line west of Mill Hill East, which had been retained for freight, closed on June 1st, 1964 and was abandoned. Part of the route is now the Parkland Walk.

MAP 41
1921

Ticket issued at **New Barnet station** on April 9th, 1965.

Ticket from **New Southgate (for Colney Hatch) station** to *Huntingdon North* issued on February 27th, 1944. The station of origin on this ticket was opened by the GNR on August 7th, 1850 as *Colney Hatch & Southgate*, renamed as *Southgate & Colney Hatch* on February 1st, 1855, as *New Southgate & Colney Hatch* on October 1st, 1876, as *New Southgate for Colney Hatch* on March 1st, 1883, as *New Southgate and Friern Barnet* by the LNER on May 1st, 1923 and as *New Southgate* by BR on March 18th, 1971. The irony is that, amongst this plethora of names, the one on this ticket was dispensed with some twenty one years previously.

New Southgate station on September 30th, 1973.
Alan Young

Looking north at **Oakleigh Park station** on March 21st, 1973.
Alan Young

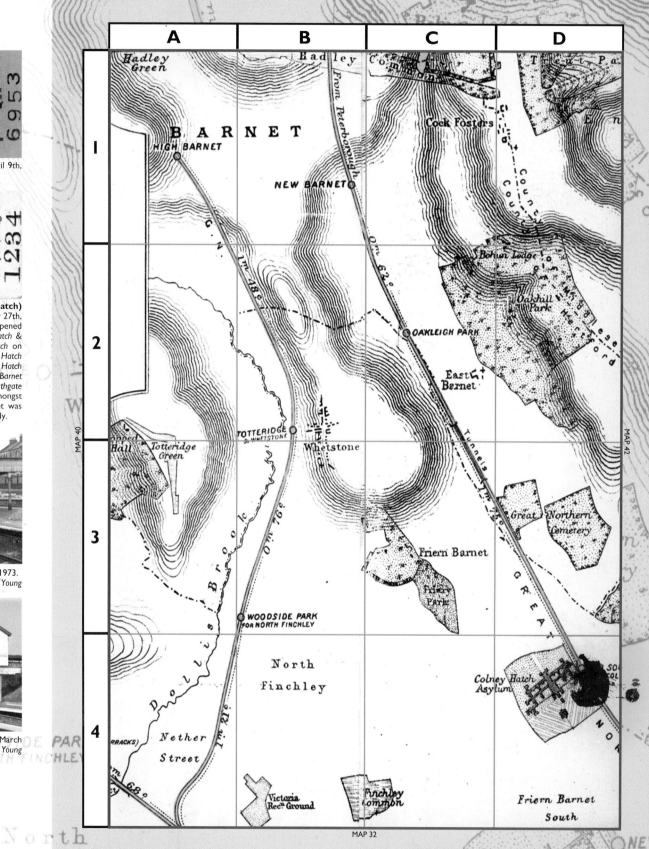

	A	B	C	D	

HIGH BARNET

NEW BARNET

COCKFOSTERS

COCKFOSTERS
DEPOT

OAKLEIGH PARK

TOTTERIDGE & WHETSTONE

WOODSIDE PARK

NEW SOUTHGATE

WEST FINCHLEY

MAP 40A

MAP 42A

MAP 32A

The entrance to **High Barnet tube station** on April 2nd, 2016. The station was opened by the GNR on April 1st, 1872.

Class 313 Unit No.313028 at **New Barnet station** on April 2nd, 2016. The station was opened by the GNR on August 7th, 1850 as *Barnet* and renamed as *New Barnet* on May 1st, 1884.

Oakleigh Park station viewed on April 2nd, 2016. It was opened by the GNR on December 1st, 1873.

A 1995 Tube Stock train, with car No.51597 leading, entering **Woodside Park tube station** on April 2nd, 2016. It was opened by the GNR on April 1st, 1872 as *Torrington Park*, renamed as *Torrington Park, Woodside* on May 1st, 1872 and as *Woodside Park* on May 1st, 1882.

MAP 42
1921

Enfield Town MPD viewed on July 13th, 1958 with Ex-LNER Class N7/5 No.69670 at the head of a queue of engines parked on the shed road. The depot was opened by the GER in 1869 and closed by BR on November 30th, 1960 when EMUs took over the passenger services. *KCH Fairey*

A ticket for a journey from **Winchmore Hill station** to *Cuffley & Goffs Oak* issued on September 20th, 1968. *Winchmore Hill* was opened by the GNR on April 1st, 1871.

Birmingham/Sulzer Type 2 (Later Class 26) Diesel Electric Bo-Bo No.**D5301** at **Enfield Chase station** in c1959. *J Joyce/Online Transport Archive*

A ticket from **Enfield Chase station** issued on June 10th, 1965.

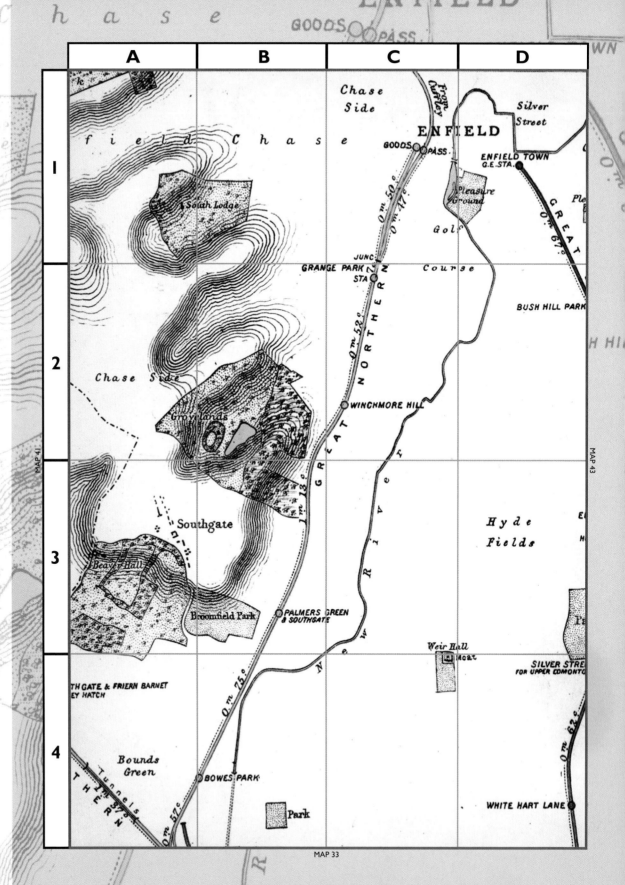

MAP 33

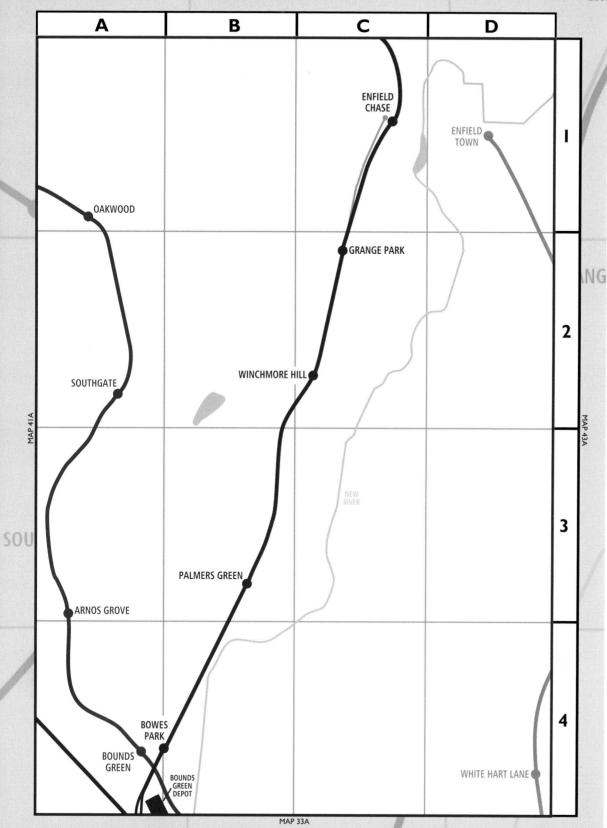

Class 313 EMU No.313037 at **Enfield Chase station** on April 2nd, 2016. The station was opened by the GNR on April 4th, 1910 as *Enfield* and replaced the original one that existed prior to the extension of the line and became the goods depot. It was renamed as *Enfield Chase* by the LNER on July 1st, 1923.

Enfield Town station on April 2nd, 2016 with Class 315 EMU No.315815 awaiting to depart. The station was opened by the Eastern Counties Railway on March 1st, 1849 as *Enfield* and renamed as *Enfield Town* by the GER on April 1st, 1866.

The entrance to the Grade II listed **Bounds Green Underground station** viewed on July 2nd, 2016. It was opened by the London Electric Railway on September 19th, 1932.

Looking south at **Palmers Green station** on July 2nd, 2016. It was opened in April 1871 by the GNR as *Palmers Green*, renamed as *Palmers Green and Southgate* on October 1st, 1876 and reverted back to *Palmers Green* by BR on May 3rd, 1971.

MAP 43
1921

A ticket issued on August 14th, 1967 for a journey from **Lower Edmonton station** to *Silver Street*. The former station was opened by the GER on July 22nd, 1872 as *Edmonton Green* and renamed as *Lower Edmonton (High Level)* on July 1st, 1883. The suffix was dropped after the closure of the *Low Level* station (*See Note* **A** *in the Legend on Map 43A*) and reverted back to *Edmonton Green* by BR on September 28th, 1992.

An unidentified Class 37 locomotive heading south through **Lower Edmonton station** on July 27th, 1975.
Alan Young

Angel Road station viewed in c1962. It was opened by the Northern & Eastern Railway on September 15th, 1840 as *Edmonton*, renamed as *Water Lane* by the Eastern Counties Railway on March 1st, 1849 and as *Angel Road* by the GER on January 1st, 1864.
Alan Young Collection

Brimsdown station, viewed from a passing train on June 18th, 1973.
Alan Young

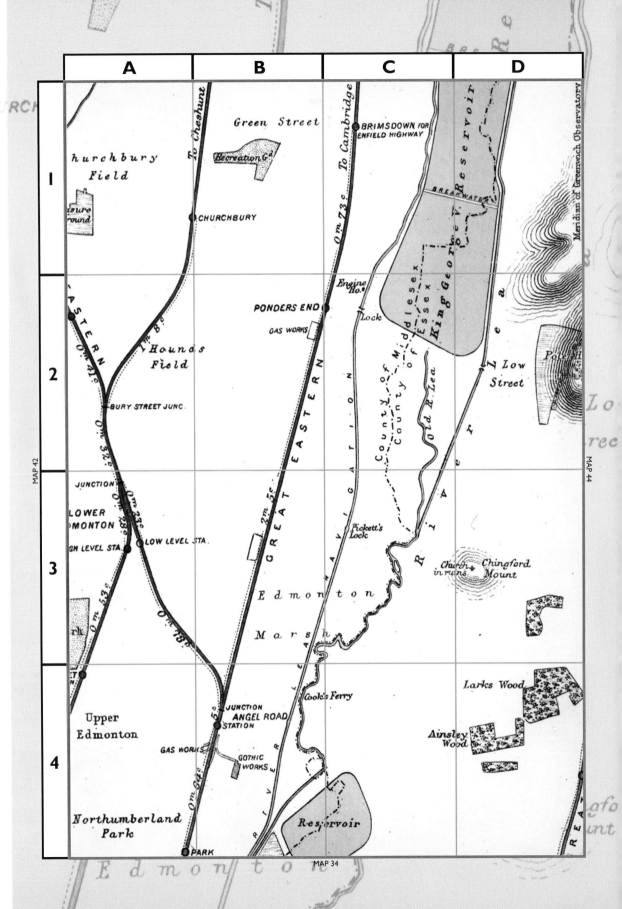

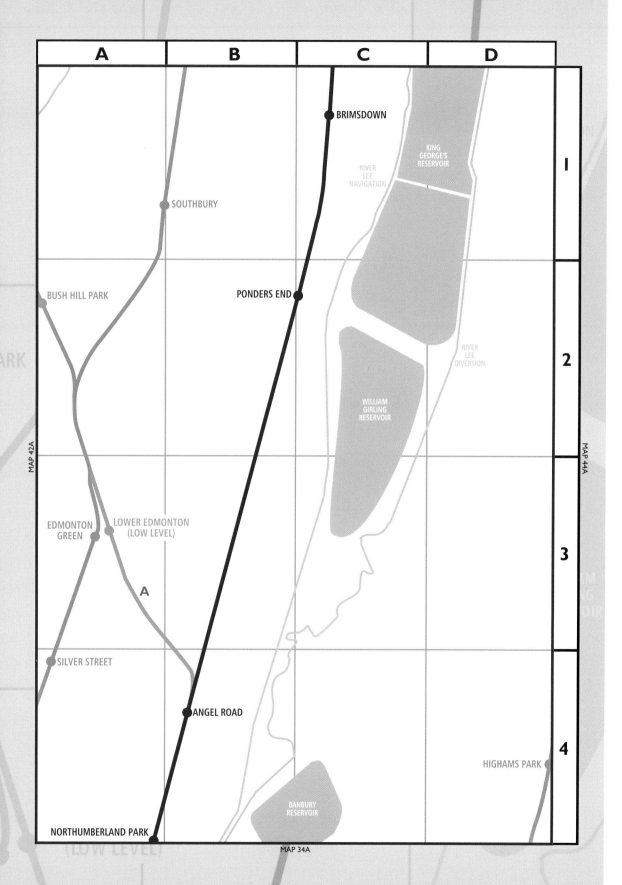

	A	B	C	D	
			BRIMSDOWN	KING GEORGE'S RESERVOIR	1
		SOUTHBURY	RIVER LEE NAVIGATION		
	BUSH HILL PARK	PONDERS END		RIVER LEE DIVERSION	2
			WILLIAM GIRLING RESERVOIR		
	EDMONTON GREEN	LOWER EDMONTON (LOW LEVEL)			3
	SILVER STREET	A			
		ANGEL ROAD		HIGHAMS PARK	4
	NORTHUMBERLAND PARK		BANBURY RESERVOIR		

MAP 42A

MAP 44A

MAP 34A

Looking north at **Brimsdown station** on July 2nd, 2016. The station was opened by the GER on October 1st, 1884.

Bush Hill Park station on July 2nd, 2016. The station was opened by the GER on November 1st, 1880.

Looking north at **Southbury station** on July 2nd, 2016. The station was opened by the GER on October 1st, 1891 as *Churchbury*, closed on October 1st, 1909 and reopened on March 1st, 1915 for munitions workers. It was then closed again on July 1st, 1919 and the line only used for freight until it was electrified and the station was reopened by BR on November 21st, 1960 as *Southbury*.

LEGEND
CLOSED LINES
A LOWER EDMONTON (LOW LEVEL) – ANGEL ROAD

Opened by the Eastern Counties Railway on March 1st, 1849 as part of the original route from the Lea Valley Line to Enfield Town and closed to passenger traffic north of Lower Edmonton (Low Level) on August 1st, 1872. Passenger services south of the station were withdrawn by the L&NER on September 11th, 1939 and the line was closed by BR on December 7th, 1964.

MAP 44

1921

The second **Loughton station** was opened on April 24th, 1865 by the GER when the line was extended to Epping. The original station, which was opened on August 22nd, 1856 by the Eastern Counties Railway, was not on a suitable alignment and was used as a goods station. A locomotive servicing facility, consisting of a turntable, coal stage and siding, was also in operation there until about 1883.

A Central Line train to Woodford at **Roding Valley tube station** on an unknown date. The station was opened by the L&NER on February 3rd, 1936.

Marcus Eavis/Online Transport Archive

A ticket issued on April 24th, 1959 to *Highams Park & Hale End,* the next station down the line from **Chingford station**.

Woodford tube station viewed on June 18th, 1986. It was opened by the Eastern Counties Railway on August 22nd, 1856.

Alan Young

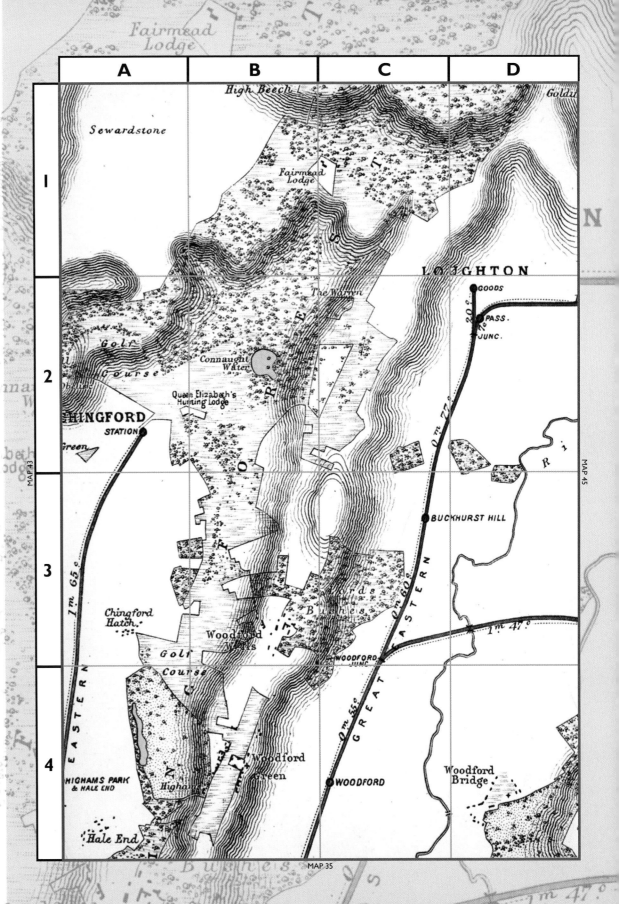

	A	B	C	D
1				
2				LOUGHTON
	CHINGFORD			
3			BUCKHURST HILL	
			RODING VALLEY	RIVER RODING
4			WOODFORD	

MAP 43A

MAP 45A

MAP 35A

Class 315 EMU No.315813 at **Chingford station** on July 2nd, 2016. The station was opened by the GNR on September 2nd, 1878 and replaced the first station, *Chingford Green,* which was opened on November 17th, 1873 and sited further south.

Loughton tube station viewed on June 19th, 2016. It is Grade II listed and was opened by the L&NER on April 28th, 1940, having replaced the original one on the site that was opened by the GER on April 4th, 1865.

Car No.91347 trailing on a train of 1992 Tube Stock at **Roding Valley tube station** on July 9th, 2016.

Looking north at **Woodford tube station** on July 9th, 2016. The station was opened by the GER on August 22nd, 1856.

MAP 45
1921

Looking east at **Chigwell tube station** on June 18th,
1921.
Alan Young

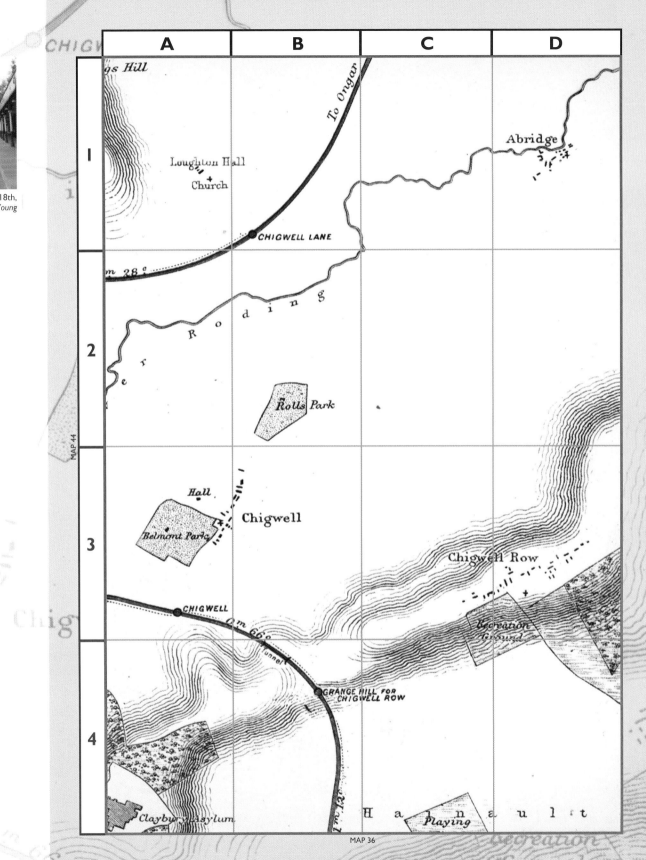

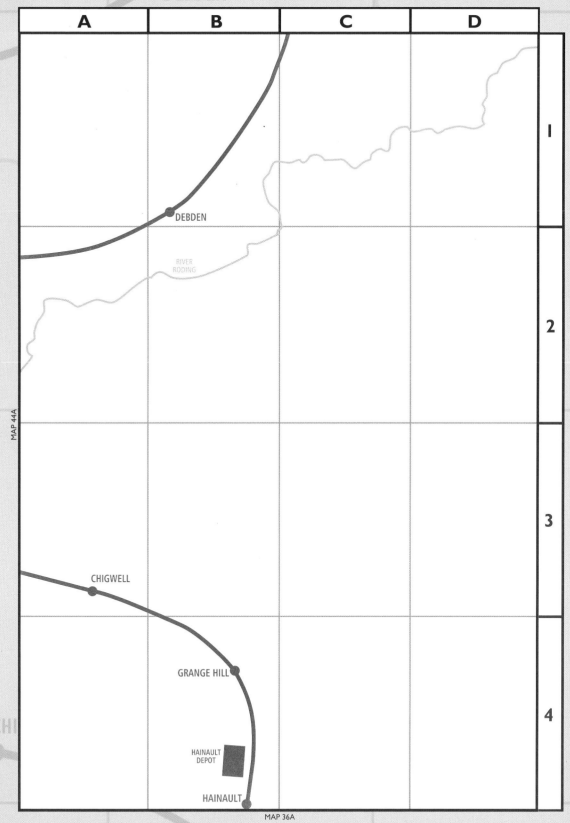

MAP 45A
January 1st, 2016

A 1992 Tube Stock train, with car No.90149 trailing, on Platform 2 at **Hainault tube station** on April 19th, 2014. The station was opened by the GER on May 1st, 1903 as a speculative venture to stimulate suburban growth but closed on October 1st, 1908 when the hoped-for passenger numbers failed to materialize. It was reopened by the L&NER on March 3rd, 1930 and transferred to LTE Central Line on May 31st, 1948.

Looking north at **Debden tube station** on July 9th, 2016. The station was opened by the GER on April 24th, 1865 as *Chigwell Road* and renamed as *Chigwell Lane* on December 1st, 1865. It was closed on May 22nd, 1916, reopened on February 3rd, 1919 and renamed as *Debden* by the LTE on September 25th, 1949.

Chigwell tube station, viewed on July 9th, 2016. The station was opened by the GER on May 1st, 1903.

Looking north at **Grange Hill tube station** on July 9th, 2016. It was opened by the GER on May 1st, 1903.

MAP 44A

DEBDEN

RIVER RODING

DEBDEN

CHIGWELL

GRANGE HILL

HAINAULT DEPOT

HAINAULT

MAP 36A

CHI

GAZETTEER 1 - 1921 Maps

Map references of stations on the "Then" maps, indexed alphabetically letter by letter.

Abbey Wood 27 4D
Acton (GW) 22 2A
Acton 22 3A
Acton Town 21 3D
Addiscombe Road 6 3D
Addison Road 22 3D
Aldergate Street 24 2C
Aldgate 24 2D
Aldgate East 24 2D
Aldwych 24 2B
Alexandra Palace 33 1A
Alperton for Perivale 21 1C
Anerley 7 1A
Angel 24 1B
Angel Road 43 4B
Ashford 10 3A

Baker Street 23 2C
Balham & Upper Tooting 14 3D
Bank 24 2C
Barking 27 1A
Barking Side 36 2B
Barnes 13 2B
Barnes Bridge 13 1B
Barons Court 22 4D
Bath Road Halt 22 4B
Battersea 14 2A
Battersea Park 14 1D
Beckenham 7 1C
Beckenham Hill 16 4D
Beckton 27 2A
Beddington Lane 5 3D
Bellingham 16 4D
Belsize Park 32 4C
Bethnal Green (GER) 25 2A
Bethnal Green (LPTB) 25 2A
Bickley 8 2C
Bingham Road Halt 6 3D
Bishopsgate 24 2D
Blackfriars 24 3B

Blackfriars Bridge 24 3B
Blackheath 17 2A
Blackheath Hill 16 1D
Blackhorse Road 34 1B
Blackwall 26 3A
Bond Street 23 2D
Borough 24 3C
Boston Manor for Brentford & Hanwell 21 4B
Bow 25 1C
Bow Road (GE) 25 1C
Bow Road (WBJ) 25 2C
Bowes Park 42 4B
Brentford 21 4B
Brentham for North Ealing 21 1C
Brimsdown for Enfield Highway 43 1C
British Museum 24 2A
Brixton 15 2B
Broad Street 24 2D
Broadway 22 4C
Brockley 16 2B
Brockley Lane 16 2B
Bromley North 8 1B
Bromley South 8 2B
Brompton Road 23 3C
Brondesbury Park 22 1D
Bruce Grove 33 1D
Buckhurst Hill 44 3C
Burdett Road 25 2C
Bushey & Oxhey 38 2B
Bush Hill Park 43 2A

Caledonian Road 33 4B
Caledonian Road & Barnsbury 33 4B
Camberwell 15 1C
Cambridge Heath 25 1A
Camden Chalk Farm 32 4C
Camden Road 32 4D
Camden Town 23 1D
Canning Town 26 2A
Cannon Street 24 3C

Canonbury 33 4C
Carpenders Park 38 3B
Carshalton 5 4C
Castlebar Park Halt 21 2A
Catford 16 3C
Catford Bridge 16 3C
Central 26 3D
Chalk Farm 32 4C
Chancery Lane 24 2B
Charing Cross 24 3A
Charlton 26 4B
Chelsea & Fulham 14 2A
Chigwell 45 3A
Chigwell Lane 45 1B
Chingford 44 2A
Chiselhurst & Bickley Park 8 2D
Chiswick for Grove Park 13 1A
Chiswick Park 22 4A
Churchbury 43 1A
City Road 24 1C
Clapham Common 15 2A
Clapham Junction 14 2C
Clapham Road 15 2A
Clapton 34 3A
Claygate for Claremont 2 4D
Clock House 7 1B
Coborn Road for Old Ford 25 1C
Connaught Road 26 3C
Coombe Lane 6 4D
Covent Garden 24 2A
Cranley Gardens 32 2D
Cricklewood 31 3D
Crofton Park 16 2B
Crouch End 33 2A
Crouch Hill 33 2B
Croxley Green 37 1C
Crystal Palace & Upper Norwood 15 4D
Custom House 26 3B

Dagenham Dock 27 1D
Dalston Junction 33 4D
Denmark Hill 15 2C
Deptford 16 1C

Dollis Hill 31 4B
Dover Street 23 3D
Down Street 23 3D
Drayton Green Halt 21 2A
Drayton Park 33 4B
Dulwich 15 3C

Ealing Broadway 21 2C
Ealing Common 21 3D
Earls Court 23 4A
Earlsfield for Summers Town 14 3B
East Acton 22 2B
East Brixton 15 2B
East Croydon 6 4C
East Dulwich 15 2D
East Finchley 32 1C
East Ham 26 1D
East Putney 13 2D
Eastcote 29 2A
Eden Park 7 3C
Edgware 1st 39 4D
Edgware 2nd 39 4D
Edgware Road 23 2C
Elephant & Castle 24 4C
Eltham & Mottingham 17 3C
Eltham Street 18 3A
Elmers End 7 2B
Elmstead Woods 8 1C
Embankment 24 3A
Enfield 42 1C
Enfield Town 42 1D
Esher for Claremont 2 3D
Essex Road 24 1C
Euston 24 1A
Euston Square 24 2A

Fairlop 36 1B
Farringdon Street 24 2B
Feltham 11 3A
Fenchurch Street 24 3D
Finchley (Church End) 32 1A
Finchley Road 1st 32 4B
Finchley Road 2nd 32 4B

Finchley Road & Frognal 32 4B
Finsbury Park 33 3B
Forest Gate 35 4B
Forest Hill 16 3B
Fulwell 11 3D

Gallions 27 3A
George Lane (Woodford) 35 1B
Gillespie Road 33 3B
Gipsy Hill for Upper Norwood 15 4D
Globe Road & Devonshire Street 25 1B
Gloucester Road 23 4B
Golders Green 32 2A
Goldhawk Road 22 3C
Goodge Street 24 2A
Goodmayes 36 3D
Gospel Oak 32 4D
Grange Hill for Chigwell Row 45 4B
Grange Park 42 2C
Great Portland Street 23 2D
Greenford 29 4D
Greenwich 16 1D
Greenwich Maze Hill 26 4A
Greenwich Park 16 1D
Grove Park 17 4B
Grove Road 22 4C

Hackbridge 5 4D
Hackney 34 4A
Hackney Downs 34 4A
Haggerston 24 1D
Hammersmith 22 4C
Hammersmith & Chiswick 22 4B
Hampstead 32 4B
Hampstead Heath 32 4C
Hampton 2 1C
Hampton Court & East Molesey 2 2D
Hampton Wick 3 1B
Hanwell & Elthorne 21 2A
Harlesden 22 1A
Harlesden for West Willesden &
        Stonebridge Park 22 1A
Harringay 33 2B

Harringay Park Green Lanes 33 2C
Harrow & Wealdstone 30 1A
Harrow on the Hill 29 2D
Hatch End for Pinner 38 4C
Haydon's Road 14 4A
Hayes 8 4A
Hayes & Harlington 19 3D
Headstone Lane 38 4D
Hendon 31 2B
Herne Hill 15 2C
Heston – Hounslow 11 1C
Highams Park & Hale End 43 4D
Highbury 33 4B
Highbury & Islington 33 4B
Highgate 32 2D
High Barnet 41 1A
High Street Kensington 23 3A
High Street (Watford) 38 1A
Hither Green 17 2A
Hoe Street 34 2C
Holborn 24 2A
Holborn Viaduct 24 2B
Holland Park 22 3D
Holloway Road 33 4B
Homerton 34 4B
Honor Oak 16 3A
Honor Oak Park 16 3B
Hornsey 33 2B
Hornsey Road 33 3A
Hounslow for Whitton 11 2C
Hounslow Barracks 11 1B
Hounslow Town 11 1D
Hyde Park Corner 23 3C
Ickenham 28 3B

Ilford 36 3A
Isleworth for Spring Grove 12 1A

Junction Road 32 3D

Kempton Park 11 4A
Kennington 24 4B
Kenton 30 2B

Kensal Green 22 1C
Kensal Rise 22 1D
Kent House 7 1B
Kentish Town 32 4D
Kew Bridge 21 4D
Kew Gardens 12 1D
Kidbrooke 17 2B
Kilburn-Brondesbury 31 4D
Kilburn & Maida Vale 23 1A
Kilburn Park 23 1A
King's Cross 24 1A
Kingston 3 1C
Knightsbridge 23 3C

Ladbroke Grove 22 2D
Ladywell 16 2D
Lambeth North 24 3B
Lancaster Gate 23 3A
Latimer Road 22 2D
Lea Bridge 34 3B
Lee 17 3A
Leicester Square 24 3A
Leman Street 25 3A
Lewisham 16 2D
Lewisham Road 16 1C
Leyton 1st 34 3D
Leyton 2nd 34 3D
Leytonstone 1st 35 3A
Leytonstone 2nd 35 3A
Limehouse 25 3C
Liverpool Street 24 2D
London Bridge 24 3C
London Fields 25 1A
Lordship Lane 16 3A
Loudoun Road for Swiss Cottage 23 1B
Loughborough Junction 15 2C
Loughton 44 2D
Lower Edmonton 43 3A
Lower Sydenham 16 4C
Ludgate Hill 24 2B

Maida Vale 23 1B
Malden for Coombe 4 2A

Mansion House 24 2C
Manor Park & Little Ilford 35 4C
Manor Way 27 3A
Marble Arch 23 2C
Mark Lane 24 4C
Marlborough Road 23 1B
Maryland Point 35 4A
Marylebone 23 2C
Merton Abbey 5 1B
Merton Park 5 1A
Mildmay Park 33 4D
Mile End 25 2C
Mill Hill 40 4B
Mill Hill for Mill Hill Barracks 40 4D
Mitcham 5 2C
Mitcham Junction 5 2C
Monument 24 3C
Moorgate 24 2C
Morden 5 1A
Mornington Crescent 23 1D
Mortlake for East Sheen 13 2A
Muswell Hill 32 1D
Neasden & Kingsbury 31 4B

New Barnet 41 1B
New Beckenham 7 1C
New Cross 16 1B
New Southgate for Friern Barnet & Colney
   Hatch 41 4D
Newbury Park 36 2B
Noel Park & Wood Green 33 1B
Norbiton 3 1D
Norbury 6 1A
North Bromley 8 1B
North Ealing 21 2D
North Dulwich 15 2C
North Greenwich 25 4D
North Harrow 29 2C
North Wembley 30 3C
North Woolwich 26 3D
Northfields & Little Ealing 21 3B
Northolt 29 3A
Northolt Halt 29 4C

Northwood 37 4C
Norwood Junction 6 2D
Notting Hill Gate 23 3A
Nunhead 16 2B

Oakleigh Park 41 3C
Old Ford 25 1C
Old Kent Road & Hatcham 16 1A
Old Oak Lane Halt 22 2B
Old Street 24 2C
Orpington 9 4B
Osterley for Spring Grove 20 4D
Oval 15 1B
Oxford Circus 23 2D

Paddington 23 2B
Palace Gates 33 1B
Palmers Green & Southgate 42 3B
Park 43 4A
Park Royal 21 2D
Park Royal & Twyford Abbey 21 1D
Parson's Green 14 1A
Peckham Rye 16 1A
Penge 16 4A
Perivale Halt 21 1A
Piccadilly Circus 24 3A
Pinner 29 1B
Plaistow 26 1B
Plumstead 27 4B
Ponders End 43 2C
Praed Street 23 2B
Preston Road 30 3C
Putney 13 2D
Putney Bridge 13 1D

Queens Park 22 1D
Queens Road (Battersea) 14 1D
Queens Road (Bayswater) 23 3A
Queens Road (Kensington) 23 3B
Queens Road (Peckham) 16 1A

Ravensbourne 7 1D
Ravenscourt Park 22 4B

Rayner's Lane 29 2C
Raynes Park 4 3C
Rectory Road 34 3A
Regent's Park 23 2D
Richmond 12 2C
Richmond (New Station) 12 2C
Rickmansworth 1st 37 2A
Rickmansworth 2nd 37 2A
Rotherhithe 25 3B
Royal Oak 23 2A
Rugby Road Halt 22 3A
Ruislip 28 2D
Ruislip & Ickenham 28 3C
Ruislip Manor 28 2D
Russell Square 24 2A

St Ann's Road 33 2D
St James's Park 24 3A
St James's Street 34 2C
St John's 16 1C
St John's Wood Road 23 1C
St Margaret's 12 2B
St Mary's 25 2A
St Mary Cray 9 2C
St Pancras 24 1A
St Paul's 24 3B
St Quintin Park for Wormwood Scrubbs 22 2C
Sandy Lodge 37 3C
Selhurst 6 2C
Seven Kings 36 3C
Seven Sisters 33 2D
Shadwell 25 2A
Shadwell & St George's East 25 2A
Shepherd's Bush 22 3C
Shepperton 1 2B
Shooters Hill & Eltham Park 17 2D
Shoreditch (EL) 24 2D
Shoreditch (LNW) 24 1D
Shoreditch (NL) 24 1D
Shortlands 8 1A
Sidcup 18 4C
Silvertown 26 3C
Silver Street for Upper Edmonton 43 4A

Sloane Square 23 4C
Snaresbrook 35 2B
Somers Town 24 1A
South Acton 22 3A
South Bermondsey 25 4A
South Bromley 25 2B
South Croydon 6 4C
South Ealing 21 3C
South Harrow 30 4A
South Harrow (For Roxeth & Northolt) 29 3D
South Kensington 23 4B
South Kentish Town 32 4D
South Tottenham & Stamford Hill 33 2D
Southall 20 3C
Southfields 13 3D
Southwark Park 25 4A
Spa Road & Bermondsey 24 4D
Stamford Brook 22 4B
Stamford Hill 33 2D
Stanmore 39 4B
Stepney Green 25 2B
Stockwell 15 1A
Stoke Newington 33 3D
Stonebridge Park 30 4D
Strand 24 3A
Stratford 34 4D
Stratford Market 26 1A
Strawberry Hill 12 3A
Streatham 15 4A
Streatham Common 6 1A
Streatham Hill 15 3A
Stroud Green 33 2B
Sudbury & Harrow Road 30 4B
Sudbury Hill for Greenford Green 30 4A
Sudbury Town for Horsenden 30 4B
Sunbury 1 1D
Sundridge Park 8 1B
Surbiton 3 2C
Surrey Docks 25 4B
Sutton 5 4A
Swiss Cottage 32 4B
Sydenham 16 4A
Sydenham Hill 15 4D

Teddington for Bushy Park 12 4A
Temple 24 3B
Thames Ditton 3 3A
The Hale for Mill Hill 40 4B
Thornton Heath 6 2C
Tidal Basin 26 3B
Tooting 14 4C
Tottenham Court Road 24 2A
Tottenham Hale 34 1A
Totteridge & Whetstone 41 2B
Trafalgar Square 24 3A
Trumper's Crossing Halt 20 3D
Tufnell Park 32 4D
Tulse Hill 15 3C
Turnham Green 22 4A
Twickenham 12 3A

Upper Holloway 33 3A
Upper Sydenham 16 4A
Upton Park 26 1C
Uxbridge Road 22 3D

Vauxhall 24 4A
Victoria 23 4D
Victoria Docks 26 3B
Victoria Park 34 4C

Waddon for Beddington & Bandon Hill 6 4B
Walham Green 14 1A
Walthamstow 24 2C
Walton for Hersham 1 4D
Walworth Road 24 4C
Wandsworth Common 14 3C
Wandsworth Town 14 2B
Wanstead Park 35 4B
Wapping 25 3A
Warren Street 23 2D
Warwick Avenue 23 2B
Waterloo 24 3B
Waterloo Junction 24 3B
Watford Junction 38 1A
Watford West 37 1D
Well Hall for North Eltham 17 3C

Welling 18 1C
Wembley for Sudbury 30 4C
Wembley Hill 30 4D
Wembley Park 30 3D
West Brompton 23 4A
West Croydon 6 3C
West Ealing 21 2B
West End Lane 32 4A
West Green 33 1C
West Ham 26 1A
West Ham South 26 2C
West Hampstead 1st 32 4A
West Hampstead 2nd 32 4A
West Harrow 29 2D
West India Dock 25 3C
West Kensington 22 4D
West Norwood 15 4C
West Wickham 7 3D
Westbourne Park 23 2A
Westcombe Park 26 4B
Westminster 24 3A

Weybridge 1 4B
White Hart Lane 42 4D
Whitechapel 25 2A
Willesden Green for Cricklewood 31 4C
Willesden Junction 22 1B
Wimbledon 13 4D
Wimbledon Park 14 4A
Winchmore Hill 42 2C
Wood Green 33 1B
Wood Lane (White City) 22 3C
Wood Street 34 2D
Woodside & South Norwood 7 3A
Woodford 44 4C
Woodgrange Park 35 4C
Woodside Park for North Finchley 41 3B
Woodstock Road Halt 22 3B
Woolwich Arsenal 27 4A
Woolwich Dockyard 26 4D
Worcester Park 4 3B

York Road 24 1A

EXTRACT FROM
BRADSHAW'S JULY 1922
RAILWAY GUIDE
Page 348
Highlighting some of the services on since-closed lines:
Broad Street to Dalston Junction
Finsbury Park - Highgate and thence to Alexandra Palace
Finchley - Edgware

GAZETTEER II - 2016 Maps

Map references of stations on the "Now" maps, indexed alphabetically letter by letter and colour coded: CLOSED, LONDON TRAMLINK, DOCKLANDS LIGHT RAILWAY, NATIONAL RAIL (inc LONDON OVERGROUND) and LONDON UNDERGROUND

Abbey Road 26A 1A
Abbey Wood 27A 4D
Acton Central 22A 3A
Acton Main Line 22A 2A
Acton Town 21A 3D
Addiscombe 6A 3D
Addiscombe Road 6A 3D
Albany Park 18A 3D
Aldgate 24A 2D
Aldgate East 24A 2D
Aldwych 24A 2B
Alexandra Palace 33A 1A
Alexandra Palace 33A 1B
All Saints 25A 2D
Alperton 21A 1C
Ampere 6A 4C
Ampere Way 6A 3A
Anerley 7A 1A
Angel 24A 1B
Angel Road 43A 4B
Archway 33A 3A
Arena 7A 2A
Arnos Grove 42A 3A
Arsenal 33A 3B
Ashford 10A 3A
Avenue Road 7A 1B

Baker Street 23A 2C
Balham 14A 3D
Balham 14A 3D
Bank 24A 2C
Bank 24A 2C
Barbican 24A 2C
Barking 27A 1A
Barkingside 36A 2B
Barnes 13A 2B
Barnes Bridge 13A 1B
Barons Court 22A 4D

Bath Road Halt 22A 4B
Battersea 14A 2B
Battersea Park 14A 1D
Battersea Park Road 14A 1D
Bayswater 23A 3A
Beckenham Hill 16A 4D
Beckenham Junction 7A 1C
Beckenham Junction 7A 1C
Beckenham Road 7A 1B
Beckton 27A 2A
Beckton 26A 2D
Beckton Park 26A 3D
Becontree 27A 1D
Beddington Lane 5A 3D
Belgrave Walk 5A 2B
Bellingham 16A 4D
Belmont 30A 1B
Belsize Park 32A 4C
Benton for North Ealing & Greystoke Park 21A 1C
Bermondsey 25A 4A
Berrylands 3A 2D
Bethnal Green 25A 2A
Bethnal Green 25A 2B
Bickley 8A 2C
Bingham Road 6A 3D
Bishopsgate (Low Level) 24A 2D
Birkbeck 6A 2A
Birkbeck 6A 2A
Blackfriars 24A 3B
Blackheath 17A 2A
Blackheath Hill 16A 1D
Blackhorse Lane 6A 3D
Blackhorse Road 34A 1B
Blackwall 25A 3D
Bond Street 23A 2D
Borough 24A 3C
Boston Manor 21A 4B
Bounds Green 42A 4A

Bow Church 25A 1C
Bow Road (GE) 25A 1C
Bow Road 25A 2C
Bowes Park 42A 4B
Brent Cross 31A 2C
Brentford 21A 4B
Brentford 21A 4B
Brentham for North Ealing 21A 1C
Brimsdown 43A 1C
British Museum 24A 2A
Brixton 15A 2B
Broad Street 24A 2D
Brockley 16A 2B
Brockley Lane 16A 2B
Bromley by Bow 25A 2D
Bromley North 8A 1B
Bromley South 8A 2B
Brompton Road 23A 3C
Brondesbury 32A 4A
Brondesbury Park 22A 1D
Bruce Grove 33A 1D
Buckhurst Hill 44A 3C
Burdett Road 25A 2C
Burnt Oak 31A 1A
Bushey 38A 2B
Bush Hill Park 43A 2A

Caledonian Road 33A 4B
Caledonian Road & Barnsbury 33A 4B
Camberwell 15A 1C
Cambridge Heath 25A 1A
Camden Road 32A 4D
Camden Town 23A 1D
Canada Water 25A 4B
Canary Wharf 25A 3C
Canary Wharf 25A 3C
Canning Town 26A 2A
Canning Town 26A 2A
Cannon Street 24A 3C
Canonbury 33A 4C
Canons Park 39A 4C
Carpenders Park 38A 3B
Carshalton 5A 4C

Castle Bar Park 21A 2A
Catford 16A 3C
Catford Bridge 16A 3C
Central 26A 3D
Chalk Farm 32A 4C
Chalk Farm 32A 4C
Chancery Lane 24A 2B
Charing Cross 24A 3A
Charlton 26A 4B
Chelsea & Fulham 14A 2A
Chessington North 3A 4C
Chigwell 45A 3A
Chingford 44A 2A
Chiselhurst 8A 2D
Chiswick 13A 1A
Chiswick Park 22A 4A
Church Street 6A 4C
City Thameslink 24A 2B
City Road 24A 1C
Clapham Common 15A 2A
Clapham High Street 15A 2A
Clapham Junction 14A 2C
Clapham North 15A 2A
Clapham South 14A 2D
Clapton 34A 3A
Claygate 2A 4D
Clock House 7A 1B
Coborn Road 25A 1C
Cockfosters 41A 1D
Colindale 31A 1B
Colliers Wood 5A 1B
Connaught Road 26A 3C
Coombe Lane 6A 4D
Covent Garden 24A 2A
Cranley Gardens 32A 2D
Cricklewood 31A 3D
Crofton Park 16A 2B
Crossharbour 25A 4D
Crouch End 33A 2A
Crouch Hill 33A 2B
Croxley 37A 1B
Croxley Green 37A 1C
Crystal Palace 6A 1D

Crystal Palace (High Level) 15A 4D
Custom House 26A 3B
Custom House 26A 3B
Cutty Sark 25A 4D
Cyprus 26A 3D

Dagenham Dock 27A 1D
Dalston Kingsland 33A 4D
Dalston Junction 33A 4D
Debden 45A 1B
Denmark Hill 15A 2C
Deptford 16A 1C
Deptford Bridge 16A 1C
Devons Road 25A 2C
Dollis Hill 31A 4B
Down Street 23A 3D
Drayton Green 21A 2A
Drayton Park 33A 4B
Dundonald Road 4A 1D

Ealing Broadway 21A 2C
Ealing Common 21A 3D
Earls Court 23A 4A
Earlsfield 14A 3B
East Acton 22A 2B
East Brixton 15A 2B
East Croydon 6A 4C
East Croydon 6A 4C
East Dulwich 15A 2D
East Finchley 32A 1C
East Ham 26A 1D
East India 25A 3D
East Putney 13A 2D
Eastcote 29A 2A
Eden Park 7A 3C
Edgware 39A 4D
Edgware (GNR) 39A 4D
Edgware Road 23A 2C
Edgware Road (Met) 23A 2C
Edmonton Green 43A 3A
Elephant & Castle 24A 4C
Elmers End 7A 2B
Elmers End 7A 2B

Elmstead Woods 8A 1C
Elstree & Borehamwood 39A D1
Eltham 17A 2C
Eltham Park 17A 2D
Elverson Road 16A 1D
Embankment 24A 3A
Enfield Chase 42A 1C
Enfield Town 42A 1D
Esher 2A 3D
Essex Road 24A 1C
Euston 24A 1A
Euston Square 24A 2A

Fairlop 36A 1B
Falconwood 18A 2A
Farringdon 24A 2B
Feltham 11A 3A
Fenchurch Street 24A 3D
Finchley Central 32A 1A
Finchley Road 32A 4B
Finchley Road 32A 4B
Finchley Road & Frognal 32A 4B
Finsbury Park 33A 3B
Forest Gate 35A 4B
Forest Hill 16A 3B
Fulwell 11A 3D
Fulham Broadway 14A 1A

Gallions 27A 3A
Gallions Reach 27A 3A
Gants Hill 36A 2A
George Street 6A 4C
Gipsy Hill 15A 4D
Globe Road & Devonshire Street 25A 1B
Gloucester Road 23A 4B
Golders Green 32A 2A
Goldhawk Road 22A 3C
Goodge Street 24A 2A
Goodmayes 36A 3D
Gospel Oak 32A 4D
Grange Hill 45A 4B
Grange Park 42A 2C
Great Portland Street 23A 2D
Green Park 23A 3D

Greenford 29A 4D
Greenwich 16A 1D
Greenwich 16A 1D
Greenwich Park 16A 1D
Grove Park 17A 4B
Grove Road 22A 4C
Gunnersbury 21A 4D

Hackbridge 5A 4D
Hackney Central 34A 4A
Hackney Downs 34A 4A
Hackney Wick 34A 4C
Haggerston 24A 1D
Hainault 45A 4B
Hammersmith 22A 4C
Hammersmith (Met/GWR) 22A 4C
Hammersmith & Chiswick 22A 4B
Hampstead 32A 4B
Hampstead Heath 32A 4C
Hampton 2A 1C
Hampton Court 2A 2D
Hampton Wick 3A 1B
Hanger Lane 21A 2C
Hanwell 21A 2A
Harlesden 22A 1A
Harringay 33A 2B
Harringay Green Lanes 33A 2C
Harrington Road 7A 2A
Harrow & Wealdstone 30A 1A
Harrow on the Hill 30A 1A
Hatch End 38A 4C
Hatton Cross 10A 1D
Haydon's Road 14A 4A
Hayes 8A 4A
Hayes & Harlington 19A 3D
Headstone Lane 38A 4D
Heathrow Junction 19A B3
Heathrow Terminals 2 & 3 10A 2B
Heathrow Terminal 4 10A 2B
Heathrow Terminal 5 10A Insert
Hendon 31A 2B
Hendon Central 31A 2C
Herne Hill 15A 2C

Heron Quays 25A 3C
Hersham 2A 4B
High Barnet 41A 1A
High Street Kensington 23A 3A
Highams Park 43A 4D
Highbury & Islington 33A 4B
Highgate 32A 2D
Highgate Low Level 32A 4D
Hillingdon 28A 4B
Hillingdon 1st 28A 4B
Hinchley Wood 3A 4A
Hither Green 17A 2A
Holborn 24A 2A
Holborn Viaduct 24A 2B
Holborn Viaduct (Low Level) 24A 2B
Holland Park 22A 3D
Holloway Road 33A 4B
Homerton 34A 4B
Honor Oak 16A 3A
Honor Oak Park 16A 3B
Hornsey 33A 2B
Hornsey Road 33A 3A
Hounslow 11A 2C
Hounslow Barracks 11A 1B
Hounslow Central 11A 1C
Hounslow East 11A 1D
Hounslow West 11A 1B
Hoxton 24A 1D
Hyde Park Corner 23A 3C
Ickenham 28A 3B

Ilford 36A 3A
Imperial Wharf 14A 1B
Island Gardens (1st) 25A 4D
Island Gardens 25A 4D
Isleworth 12A 1A

Junction Road 32A 3D

Kempton Park 11A 4A
Kennington 24A 4B
Kensal Green 22A 1C
Kensal Rise 22A 1D

Kensington Olympia 22A 3D
Kent House 7A 1B
Kentish Town 32A 4D
Kentish Town West 32A 4D
Kenton 30A 2B
Kew Bridge 21A 4D
Kew Gardens 12A 1D
Kidbrooke 17A 2B
Kilburn 31A 4D
Kilburn High Road 23A 1A
Kilburn Park 23A 1A
King George V 26A 3D
King's Cross 24A 1A
King's Cross Thameslink 24A 1B
King's Cross - St Pancras 24A 1A
Kingsbury 30A 2D
Kingston 3A 1C
Knightsbridge 23A 3C
Ladbroke Grove 22A 2D

Ladywell 16A 2D
Lambeth North 24A 3B
Lancaster Gate 23A 3A
Langdon Road 25A 2D
Latimer Road 22A 2D
Lea Bridge 34A 3B
Lebanon Road 6A 4D
Lee 17A 3A
Leicester Square 24A 3A
Leman Street 25A 3A
Lewisham 16A 2D
Lewisham 16A 2D
Lewisham Road 16A 1C
Leyton 34D 3D
Leyton Midland Road 34A 3D
Leytonstone 35A 3A
Leytonstone High Road 35A 3A
Limehouse (1st) 25A 3C
Limehouse 25A 2B
Limehouse 25A 2B
Liverpool Street 24A 2D
London Bridge 24A 3C
London City Airport 26A 3C

London Fields 25A 1A
Lord's 23A 1C
Lordship Lane 16A 3A
Loughborough Junction 15A 2C
Loughton 44A 2D
Lower Edmonton (Low Level) 43A 3A
Lower Sydenham 16A 4C
Ludgate Hill 24A 2B

Maida Vale 23A 1B
Maiden Lane 33A 4A
Malden Manor 4A 3A
Mansion House 24A 2C
Manor House 33A 2C
Manor Park 35A 4C
Manor Way 27A 3A
Marble Arch 23A 2C
Mark Lane 24A 4C
Marlborough Road 23A 1B
Maryland 35A 4A
Marylebone 23A 2C
Maze Hill 26A 4A
Merton Abbey 5A 1B
Merton Park 5A 1A
Mildmay Park 33A 4D
Mile End 25A 2C
Mill Hill Broadway 40A 4B
Mill Hill (The Hale) 40A 4B
Mill Hill East 40A 4D
Mitcham (1st) 5A 2C
Mitcham (2nd) 5A 2C
Mitcham Eastfields 5A 1D
Mitcham Junction 5A 2C
Mitcham Junction 5A 2C
Monument 24A 3C
Moor Park 37A 3C
Moorgate 24A 2C
Morden 5A 2A
Morden Road 5A 1A
Morden South 5A 2A
Mornington Crescent 23A 1D
Mortlake 13A 2A
Motspur Park 4A 2C

Motteringham 17A 3C
Mudchute 25A 4D
Muswell Hill 32A 1D

Neasden 31A 4B
Necropolis 24A 3B
New Barnet 41A 1B
New Beckenham 7A 1C
New Cross 16A 1C
New Cross Gate 16A 1B
New Eltham 18A 3A
New Malden 4A 2B
New Southgate 41A 4D
Newbury Park 36A 2B
Noel Park & Wood Green 33A 1B
Norbiton 3A 1D
Norbury 6A 1A
North Acton 22A 2A
North Ealing 21A 2D
North Dulwich 15A 2C
North Greenwich 26A 3A
North Greenwich 25A 4D
North Harrow 29A 2C
North Sheen 12A 2D
North Wembley 30A 3C
North Woolwich 26A 3D
Northfields 21A 3B
Northolt 29A 4C
Northolt Halt 29A 4C
Northolt Park 29A 3C
Northumberland Park 43A 4A
Northwick Park 30A 2B
Northwood 37A 4C
Northwood Hills 28A 1D
Norwood Junction 6A 2D
Notting Hill Gate 23A 3A
Nunhead 16A 2B

Oakleigh Park 41A 3C
Oakwood 42A 1A
Old Ford 25A 1C
Old Kent Road & Hatcham 16A 1A
Old Oak Lane Halt 22A 2B

Old Street 24A 2C
Orpington 9A 4B
Osterley 20A 4D
Oval 15A 1B
Oxford Circus 23A 2D

Paddington 23A 2B
Paddington 23A 2B
Paddington (Met) 23A 2B
Palace Gates Wood Green 33A 1B
Palmers Green 42A 3B
Park Royal 21A 2D
Park Royal (GWR) 21A 2D
Park Royal & Twyford Abbey 21A 1D
Park Royal West Halt 21A 1D
Parson's Green 14A 1A
Peckham Rye 16A 1A
Penge East 16A 4A
Penge West 7A 1A
Perivale 21A 1B
Perivale Halt 21A 1A
Petts Wood 9A 2A
Phipps Bridge 5A 2B
Piccadilly Circus 24A 3A
Pimlico 24A 1D
Pinner 29A 1B
Plaistow 26A 1B
Plumstead 27A 4B
Ponders End 43A 2C
Pontoon Dock 26A 3B
Poplar 25A 3D
Preston Road 30A 3C
Preston Road (1st) 30A 3C
Prince Regent 26A 3B
Pudding Mill Lane 25A 1D
Putney 13A 2D
Putney Bridge 13A 1D

Queens Park 22A 1D
Queens Road (Peckham) 16A 1A
Queenstown Road (Battersea) 14A 1D
Queensbury 30A 1D
Queensway 23A 3B

Ravensbourne 7A 1D
Ravenscourt Park 22A 4B
Rayner's Lane 29A 2C
Raynes Park 4A 1C
Rectory Road 34A 3A
Redbridge 35A 2C
Reeves Corner 6A 4B
Regent's Park 23A 2D
Richmond 12A 2C
Rickmansworth 37A 2A
Rickmansworth (Church Street) 37A 2A
Roding Valley 44A 3C
Rotherhithe 25A 3B
Royal Albert 26A 3C
Royal Oak 23A 2A
Royal Victoria 26A 3B
Rugby Road Halt 22A 3A
Ruislip 28A 2D
Ruislip Gardens 28A 3D
Ruislip Manor 28A 2D
Russell Square 24A 2A

St Ann's Road 33A 2D
St James's Park 24A 3A
St James Street Walthamstow 34A 2C
St John's 16A 1C
St John's Wood 23A 1B
St Helier 5A 2A
St Margaret's 12A 2B
St. Mary's 25A 2A
St Mary Cray 9A 2C
St Pancras International 24A 1A
St Paul's 24A 3B
St Quintin Park for Wormwood Scrubbs 22A 2C
Sandilands 6A 4D
Selhurst 6A 2C
Seven Kings 36A 3C
Seven Sisters 33A 2D
Shadwell 25A 2A
Shadwell 25A 2A
Shadwell 25A 3A
Shepherd's Bush 22A 3D
Shepherd's Bush (LSWR) 22A 3C

Shepherd's Bush (WLR) 22A 3D
Shepherd's Bush Market 22A 3D
Shepperton 1A 2B
Shoreditch (ELR) 24A 2D
Shoreditch High Street 24A 1D
Shoreditch (NLR) 24A 1D
Shortlands 8A 1A
Sidcup 18A 4C
Silvertown 26A 3C
Silver Street 43A 4A
Sloane Square 23A 4C
Snaresbrook 35A 2B
South Acton 22A 3A
South Bermondsey (1st) 25A 4A
South Bermondsey 25A 4A
South Bromley 25A 2D
South Croydon 6A 4C
South Docks 25A 3D
South Ealing 21A 3C
South Greenford 21A 1A
South Harrow 29A 3D
South Harrow (1st) 29A 3D
South Hampstead 23A 1B
South Kensington 23A 4B
South Kentish Town 32A 4D
South Kenton 30A 3B
South Merton 4A 2D
South Quay (1st) 25A 3C
South Quay 25A 3D
South Ruislip 29A 3A
South Tottenham 33A 2D
South Wimbledon 5A 1A
South Woodford 35A 1B
Southall 20A 3C
Southbury 43A 1A
Southfields 13A 3D
Southgate 42A 2A
Southwark 24A 3B
Southwark Park 25A 4A
Spa Road & Bermondsey 24A 4D
Stamford Brook 22A 4B
Stamford Hill 33A 2D
Stanmore 39A 3C

Stanmore Village 39A 4B
Star Lane 26A 2A
Stepney Green 25A 2B
Stockwell 15A 1A
Stoke Newington 33A 3D
Stonebridge Park 30A 4D
Stoneleigh 4A 4B
Stratford 34A 4D
Stratford International 34A 4D
Stratford High Street 26A 1A
Strawberry Hill 12A 3A
Streatham 15A 4A
Streatham Common 6A 1A
Streatham Hill 15A 3A
Stroud Green 33A 2B
Sudbury & Harrow Road 30A 4B
Sudbury Hill 30A 4A
Sudbury Hill Harrow 30A 4A
Sudbury Town 30A 4B
Sunbury 1A 1D
Sundridge Park 8A 1B
Surbiton 3A 2C
Surrey Quays 25A 4B
Sutton 5A 4A
Sutton Common 5A 4A
Swiss Cottage 32A 4B
Sydenham 16A 4A
Sydenham Hill 15A 4D
Syon Lane 12A 1A

Teddington 12A 4A
Temple 24A 3B
Thames Ditton 3A 3A
Therapia Park 6A 3A
Thornton Heath 6A 2C
Tidal Basin 26A 3B
Tolworth 3A 4D
Tooting 14A 4C
Tooting 14A 4C
Tooting Bec 14A 3C
Tooting Broadway 14A 4C
Tottenham Court Road 24A 2A
Tottenham Hale 34A 1A

Totteridge & Whetstone 41A 2B
Tower Gateway 24A 3D
Tower Hill 24A 3D
Trumper's Crossing Halt 20A 3D
Tufnell Park 32A 4D
Tulse Hill 15A 3B
Turnham Green 22A 4A
Turnpike Lane 33A 1B
Twickenham (1st) 12A 3A
Twickenham 12A 3A

Upney 27A 1B
Upper Halliford 1A 1C
Upper Holloway 33A 3A
Upper Sydenham 16A 4A
Upton Park 26A 1C
Uxbridge Road 22A 3D

Vauxhall 24A 4A
Victoria 23A 4D
Victoria Park 34A 4C

Waddon 6A 4B
Waddon Marsh (1st) 6A 4B
Waddon Marsh (2nd) 6A 4B
Walthamstow Central 24A 2C
Walthamstow Queen's Road 24A 2C
Walton on Thames 1A 4D
Walworth Road 24A 4C
Wandle Park 6A 4B
Wandsworth Common 14A 3C
Wandsworth Road 14A 1D
Wandsworth Town 14A 2B
Wanstead 35A 2B
Wanstead Park 35A 4B
Wapping 25A 3A
Warren Street 23A 2D
Warwick Avenue 23A 2B
Waterloo 24A 3B
Waterloo East 24A 3B
Watford 38A 1D
Watford High Street 38A 1A
Watford Junction 38A 1A

BIBLIOGRAPHY

Railway Atlas - Then and Now 2nd Edition, Paul Smith & Keith Turner. Ian Allan ISBN 9 780711 038332
London Railway Atlas 4th Edition, Joe Brown. Ian Allan ISBN 9 780711 038196
The Directory of Railway Stations, RVJ Butt. Patrick Stevens Ltd ISBN 1 85260 508 1
The Directory of British Engine Sheds and Principal Locomotive Servicing Points: 1, Roger Griffiths & Paul Smith. Oxford Publishing Company ISBN 0 86093 542 6
Railway Passenger Stations in Great Britain: A Chronology - 3rd Edition 2005, Michael Quick. Railway & Canal Historical Society ISBN 978 0 901461 57 5
Bradshaw's July 1922 Railway Guide. Guild Publishing London (Reprinted 1985)
Also accessed, the Disused Stations website at http://www.disused-stations.org.uk

WITH THANKS TO

John Alsop, Tony Booth, Graham Larkbey, John Ledward, Phil Mackie, Philip Stuart, Keith Turner, Peter Waller, Alan Young and John Atkinson for his generous loan of the original maps.

LONDON, HARROW AND WEALDSTONE, and STANMORE.—London and North Western.

Week Days only.

EXTRACT FROM BRADSHAW'S JULY 1922 RAILWAY GUIDE
Page 435
Highlighting the services on a since-closed line:
Harrow & Wealdstone - Stanmore Village

LONDON, WATFORD, CROXLEY GREEN, and RICKMANSWORTH (One class only).
London and North Western.

EXTRACT FROM BRADSHAW'S JULY 1922 RAILWAY GUIDE
Page 427
Highlighting the services on since-closed lines:
Watford Junction - Rickmansworth (Church Street) and
Watford Junction - Croxley Green